VIETNAM NURSE

MENDING & REMEMBERING

To: JoAnn
Let us never
forget that women
served too!

Peace ~
Love

7/7/2015

VIETNAM NURSE

MENDING & REMEMBERING

LOU EISENBRANDT

Deeds Publishing | Atlanta

Published by Deeds Publishing in Athens, GA
www.deedspublishing.com

Printed in The United States of America

Library of Congress Cataloging-in-Publications Data is available upon
request.

ISBN 978-1-941165-68-3

Books are available in quantity for promotional or premium use. For
information, email info@deedspublishing.com.

First Edition, 2015

10 9 8 7 6 5 4 3 2 1

I dedicate this book to my husband, Jim; my daughter, Jen, and her husband, Matt; and my son, Matt, and his wife, Gen; for listening to my war stories over and over through the years. In addition, they have supported me as I refuse to allow Parkinson's Disease to rule my life. To my family including my siblings Rita, Wayne, and Ivan who have been with me through this long journey.

In memory of Mom, Dad, and brother Denny.

I also dedicate this book to the many courageous Army nurses who cared for wounded and dying servicemen as well as injured Vietnamese citizens during the Vietnam War. Most of us received few medals of recognition for our service and many are still waiting to hear the words "Welcome home!"

CONTENTS

REMEMBER

Remember the sounds of death
*   the gurgle of a last breath.*
Remember helicopter blades: whop, whop, whop
*   bringing bloodied and broken bodies.*
Remember the acrid odor of burning flesh
*   and peeling skin from white phosphorus.*
Remember rain, rain, and yet more rain.
Remember the whistle of rockets, splashing in the sea
*   where earlier that day we had skied.*
Remember sand, coconut oil, guitars and music.
Remember shoulders wet from tears,
*   blood dripping on our boots,*
*   body bags cradling their silent contents.*
Remember escaping into scotch and cigarettes,
*   writing, loving, filming, laughing.*
Remember leaving whole, when so many were broken.
Remember and share, whenever you can, so that others may
*   never forget.*

WHY THE ARMY

"You were born with wanderlust in your soul!" a friend recently said to me. I chuckled, but realized that she was indeed correct. I always wanted more—more friends, more excitement, more outfits, more fun. However, the primary thing that I wanted more of was the world. More freedom to investigate and explore other countries and cultures excited me as a child. Leafing through our Encyclopedia Britannica with its burgundy vinyl covered volumes, I dreamt of seeing in person the places pictured within. There seemed to be a new adventure for each letter of the alphabet. Whenever I am asked why I joined the Army, I always give the same reply…I wanted to see the world!

It was really quite simple. Mascoutah, my home community, population 3000, when I was growing up in Southern Illinois, was located just 7 miles from Scott Air Force Base. It was a large facility that housed many Air Force families whose children attended my local high school. I developed friendships with my contemporaries who had lived in England, Italy, Germany, and other countries that seemed quite exotic to a young girl whose travel experience reached only as far as Wisconsin and Colorado. Growing up in a blue collar working society with a father who was employed at a livestock feed store to distribute feed to farmers and a stay at home mother of five, there was no money in the till to vacation abroad (which in my world included California and New York). Often I would visit my globe trotting classmates to find their homes or apartments filled with porcelain vases from Japan, cuckoo clocks from Germany, and brightly colored china from Italy. On days when we were out of school, my dad, on occasion, would allow us to ride along, sitting on the hundred pound burlap sacks, filled with grain, in the back of the truck as he delivered them to farmers. I would dream of riding in a plane or on a train far away from the dusty country lanes of Illinois. As I approached high school age, the answer to my quest for travel became more urgent with each passing day. By the time I entered nursing school my decision had taken hold. I would join the Army; I would see the world.

I was the oldest of five siblings, three brothers and a sister. Since there was an eleven-year difference between the youngest, my brother Ivan, and myself, I was often relegated to the position of "being in charge." From bathing to dressing to baby-sitting, I frequently assisted my mom in caring for the younger children. Life in Mascoutah revolved around a daily routine of laundry, cleaning, gardening, preserving fruits and vegetables, and schoolwork. We all attended the local Catholic grade school and went to Mass on Sunday. There were extracurricular activities—4H for the girls, sports for the boys, theater for my sister Rita and I, and involvement in the American Legion and its auxiliary for mom and dad. We made do with just one car, which curtailed even long weekend getaways unless everyone went along.

When I realized that there were no funds available for me to go to a four year college to study theater and music, I abandoned my desire to be a famous actress and pursued my second career choice—nursing. I remember vividly my father's objections to this plan. He felt that, since many of my hometown classmates were going directly from high school to gainful employment, there was no need to spend more money before earning it. When I was accepted into St. Joseph's School of Nursing during my senior year at Mascoutah High, however, my mom convinced him that it was the right thing for me. Located in Alton, Illinois, just 50 miles away, it was not, by today's standards, distant. Of course, with just one family car, I could only come home if someone drove to school to pick me up. As I started my studies at St. Joseph's School of Nursing, I missed seeing my family, but I was spreading my wings.

My decision to walk into the recruiting office and join the Army did not result from having a celestial vision or being struck by lightning. When I think back to why and when I got up the nerve to visit the office in nearby Belleville, Illinois, I don't recall it as a difficult decision. I simply made up my mind to go and even asked a friend to accompany me. She said that she might be interested as well, but changed her mind once we got there. I picked up the necessary forms and filled them out, which included permission from my parents. Two days later, I returned to the recruiting office with paperwork in hand, raised my right hand and swore to uphold or behave or something. It was May 1967. I was twenty years old.

Not everyone was pleased with the direction that I had chosen for my future. The nun who was the head of my nursing school, a member of the Daughters of Charity order, called me into her office to express her disappointment saying that I was "throwing my nursing career away." She seemed to think that I would not be making the best use of what I had learned during my time at St. Joseph's. She said that I had the talent to become a floor superintendent some day. Why would I give that up to work in an Army hospital? Neither of us could have imagined the extent to which my nursing education would be put to good use.

My military "duty assignment" during my senior year in nursing school was as it had been—to stay in school. I was considered to be on "active reserve status" and received a monthly paycheck to keep studying. In exchange for the stipend, I committed to serve two years on active duty. It seemed to be a perfect plan to me, two years to work and play while living in, I hoped, a faraway country. Little did I realize just how far away!

My time in nursing school was filled with new friends, hours of studying, weeks on duty in a variety of clinical areas as well as plenty of the usual college antics and nonsense. The school was small compared to most colleges, with just 26 women in our graduating class. The first male student was enrolled in the class following ours. No sports teams, cheerleaders, or sororities! Most of us were from the southern Illinois and Missouri area with only a couple ladies traveling from outside a 100-mile radius. Today, many of my fellow graduates continue to reside within those parameters. When we graduated on June 8, 1968, most in the class were heading to employment in the St. Louis/Alton area. I, on the other hand, was headed to Ft. Sam Houston, Texas for Officer's Basic Training. At graduation, as I accepted the Florence Nightingale award for the highest GPA of my class from Sr. Virginia, there was no warm smile on her face. She was still convinced that I would not be making the most of my hard work. How wrong she would be!

After graduation came state boards, which were held in Chicago and involved a class train trip to get there. Pencils in hand, we spent two days trying to remember everything that we had learned in the previous three years. I don't recall details of the test itself, but do have a vivid memory of 12 of us enjoying dinner one evening and meticulously dividing up the check by what we had actually eaten. It took forever! After all, we were poor former students and refused to pay for any morsel that we had not consumed. Returning from Chicago, we made the most of riding in a private rail car as I strummed my guitar and everyone joined in song.

My reporting date for Ft. Sam was 14 November

1968. In the intervening months, I worked at a nearby hospital in a secretarial capacity because I had not gotten word from the state licensing board decreeing me a full-fledged registered nurse. Fortunately, that bit of good news did arrive before I left for Texas.

OFFICERS BASIC TRAINING

The words "basic training" conger up images of men low crawling under barbed wire, lifting legs high while running through old tires on an obstacle course from hell and attempting to kill an imaginary enemy with an M-16 while lying on one's belly in either a puddle of mud or a swirling sandstorm. It is just that and so much more! Actually, I never had to deal with the mud but learned to shoot a .45 caliber pistol and practiced bandaging the "injured" rather than creating the injury.

Before leaving home, I heard of another adventurous nurse from a nearby town who was also to report to Ft. Sam the same day that I was. Having gotten a new Rambler American (not very sporty but definitely reliable), I offered to drive both of us down to Texas with a bit of help from her for gas money. We roomed together for the next six weeks and, as I recall, enjoyed our time together. My photos, in attempting to resurrect that time period, show groups of women in regulation dark green ill-fitting fatigues, attempting to splint arms, carry litters, bandage pretend sucking chest wounds and start IVs. Fortunately, this was all a faux war and no patients were harmed in the process.

Our first week of study was on the basics of being a soldier—military courtesies (how to salute—indoors and out), map reading (pre-GPS era), and lots of drill and command marching. I must confess that, once I left Ft. Sam, I never used a grid map to navigate nor did I pursue marching anywhere!

Week two concentrated more on nursing, specifically with an introduction to the following topics: "Military Preventive Medicine" (I can't remember if that is different from civilian preventive medicine), "Prevention and Control of Arthropod-Borne Diseases" and "The Medical Effects of Nuclear Weapons." When that was followed by a class entitled "Survival, Escape and Evasion," I started to sense that I had a good chance of being assigned somewhere other than San Francisco or Denver—the most sought after Army hospital sites in the U.S.!

During the remaining four weeks, the nursing classes covered such issues as defense against biological and chemical agents, management of common battle injuries, triage of mass casualties, and how to don a gas mask. There was even a lesson in field stripping a cigarette, a practice that I have never forgotten from my orientation at Ft. Sam. It involves tearing apart the filter when it is all that remains after smoking. The purpose is to make the cigarette filter more biodegradable and avoid leaving a trail for the enemy. To this day, it is brought to mind every time I spy a filtered butt on the ground!

It was, however, a class in the fifth week that really caught my attention. It was entitled "Patient Care Experiences in Vietnam." Not England or Germany or even stateside. Clearly we were being prepared for the very real possibility that the war zone could be our final destination. I don't remember the contents of the curriculum for the class, but I have not forgotten the title and the impact that it had.

My stay at Ft. Sam was not all work though. One weekend, my roommate and I headed south, leaving the U.S. for the first time. No passports were needed in those days to visit Mexico. We spent two days in Monterey, Mexico where my most vivid memory is that of the two of us riding donkeys up a hill in the rain. I was wearing a woven wool poncho that I had purchased as a souvenir. The combination of soggy poncho and rain soaked burro was a similar scent to wet dog odor with undertones of fried tortillas. Not the most pleasant, but definitely not one that I would ever experience back home.

In doing research for this book, I leafed through the collection of papers that I had amassed during my time in the Army such as pay vouchers, travel orders, requests for leave, and more. Nestled among the many bits of my past was a letter of recommendation that I had totally forgotten about over the last 45+ years. It was from the commandant of the U.S. Army Medical Field Service

School concerning my time in the Officer Basic Course at Ft. Sam. The commendation congratulated me for having "graduated at the top of your class" and that I was designated as the "Distinguished Honor Graduate"! My memory of that had totally faded, but I must have been better at the rifle range than I remembered!

OVER THE RIVER AND THROUGH THE WOODS

Back home in Mascoutah, I had two weeks of leave to gather my belongings and hit the road in my Rambler headed to Ft. Dix, New Jersey. This journey took me further from my home than I had ever ventured. As I was to report for duty on 2 January 1969, I spent a very snowy New Year's Eve in a roadside hotel in the Alleghenies far from any gala celebration. The reality of my having taken, "the road less traveled," to quote poet Robert Frost, set in that night. My family and classmates were partying and welcoming in a fresh year with champagne and confetti. The television in my hotel room filled the air with strains of "Auld Lang Syne" performed by Guy Lombardo and his band, the Royal Canadians. I, however, was about to embark on a journey that I could not have imagined. Alas the one memory that has stayed with me from that night was not my concern for the future, but rather thinking that the only occasion that I would have to wear my dress blues, our "fanciest" uniform, would have been while attending the base commander's New Year's Day reception. Since I was not arriving until the next day, I never had that chance. The following year, I was in Vietnam and no one considered taking dress blues to a warzone! I recall selling my uniform to someone at Ft. Dix, who might have had a need for it once a year.

Life at Walson Army Hospital on Ft. Dix gave me my first taste of what might await me should I get orders for Vietnam. The ward that I was assigned to housed a plethora of patients. The most compelling group was prisoners from the stockade on post. Their crimes ran the gamut from going AWOL to petty theft to first-degree murder. There were two MPs on duty at all times, guarding the locked door. Each shift, the head nurse (either another nurse or I) would make rounds, checking under mattresses for hidden syringes and needles, pills not consumed, as well as contraband—knives, rope, etc. One of the inmate/patients did escape by tying bed sheets together and going through a high window. I am not certain how he accomplished the aerial feat, but was relieved that he did not chose to leave while I was on duty!

The second group was injured veterans who had returned from the war zone, but whose wounds needed further attention—irrigation, antibiotics, debriding. These GI's were most grateful for their care and especially looked forward to their evening back-rubs, which helped to ease the discomfort of sore muscles. These soldiers had spent from as little as a few weeks up to a year in Vietnam. Their wounds had been serious enough to result in their evacuation from a field hospital in country to a military hospital in Europe or Asia. From there, they were sent to the medical military facility closest to their homes. They had seen the enemy and survived, though not without scars.

A third group, with wrongly perceived ideas of what it meant to be tough, was draftees who had gotten into fights at one of the local bars or in the barracks and ended up with broken jaws. For over a month after their jaws were wired shut, these patients were unable to chew and thus took their meals through straws. Their view of the war was quite different from that of the vets.

The final area of my ward was set aside for two types of potential patients. The first were draftees who came down with URIs (upper respiratory infections or serious colds). When a germ found its way into a group of young men, it spread rapidly and was difficult to control. Therefore, the guys were hospitalized to help reduce the number of infected individuals. The hacking coughs and sneezing provided a cacophony of background music for the entire ward.

It was the last group that found its way into my nursing career that made me laugh, however. In the 1970s, young men had to be a certain weight to go on active duty, even though they were drafted. The Army cleverly set up a plan to fatten up the skinnies and slim down the fatties by confining them to the same ward in the hospital and ordering specific diets. Unfortunately, they did not think the plan through as thoroughly as they should have. The result—the fatties beat up the skinnies, took their milkshakes and got fatter while the skinnies got skinnier. Not a good strategic plan, sir!

My BOQ (bachelor officers' quarters) roommate at Ft. Dix was a petite new nursing graduate, like myself, from Pennsylvania. We bonded quickly as we opened the cupboards in our new apartment and both screamed at the sight of roaches scurrying for cover. Fortunately the rest of my memories of the nine months there were a bit more pleasant. There were delicious meals at the Officers' Club, champagne to celebrate every friend's promotion, dancing on the weekends as well as an opportunity to experience and explore the East Coast. I took in a conference in Washington, D.C.; toured the historical sites of Philadelphia, and spent time in New York City when my family came to visit. We also drove to Atlantic City, discovering rum raisin ice cream on its famous boardwalk. My siblings delighted in their first chance to swim in the ocean, chilly though it was.

While at Ft. Dix, I met a young soldier who was an officer in the Corp of Engineers. We began dating and, when he was assigned to TDY (temporary duty) at Camp Drum in upstate New York, I would get weekend passes and drive north to see him. One weekend, I chose a different means of transportation and experienced my very first plane ride—on a prop plane owned by Mohawk Airlines. Sadly, I spent most of the short flight in the bathroom or bent over in my seat with the airsickness bag clasped firmly to my mouth with both hands. By the next time that I would fly, a much greater distance, my stomach was better, though still not entirely happy. Fortunately, those issues are now in the past. The sad postscript to this romance, though it continued into my time in Vietnam, is that my "boyfriend" was abusive. Luckily, I eventually saw through the excuses and apologies, ending the relationship. More about that later.

I remember well the August day that a manila envelope arrived in my mail at the BOQ. It contained a congratulatory letter informing me that I had been reassigned to a detachment in the Republic of South Vietnam. What I do not recall is my immediate reaction. Certainly I was numb, not knowing what lay ahead but I can't say that I was shocked. After all, clearly our basic training had all the implications that most of us would be headed there. In addition, when you are in the military, you are TOLD what to do, where to go, how to pack, etc. I knew that I would not have to make my own travel arrangements, locate uniforms, or worry about housing or where to eat. We were given limits on luggage and suggestions for personal items. In retrospect, we could have used so much more information, especially from a psychological aspect. All these decades later and aware of how many vets are struggling with PTSD, a class in resilience, fear, loneliness, strains on relationships from separation, and reentering the real world would have made life easier for many of us.

We were given 30 days of leave during which I drove back to Mascoutah from New Jersey, spent time with family and friends, and eventually said goodbye to all of them. On the actual day of my departure, my mother, accompanied by my youngest brother, drove me to St. Louis Lambert Field for my 8:55 a.m. flight. Many years later, I would learn that a highway patrolman stopped my mother as she returned to Mascoutah. He asked her if she knew that she was speeding, not something one would ever imagine my mother doing. She proclaimed that she thought that she was just going with the flow of the traffic and went on to explain that she had just dropped off her daughter who was an Army nurse headed to Vietnam. The officer, gazing at her misty eyes, let her be on her way, suggesting that she might pay a bit more attention to her speed for the remainder of her drive.

LEAVING "THE WORLD" BEHIND

Upon arriving in San Francisco, I boarded a bus that carted me and others to Travis Air Force Base where, after a long delay and an overnight stay, we finally boarded an American Airlines plane at 3:30 in the morning. On the plane, filled to capacity with soldiers, 13 of us were women. It was instantly clear that, as a female, I was going to have to be comfortable in a man's domain.

As I settled into my seat, I took out the new daily calendar that my roommate at Fort Dix had given me as a going away gift. The first notations I made were on that initial flight, but the recollections continued throughout the year. Looking back, I am most grateful for that little spiral notebook with its daily entries. Along with my many photographs, it helped immensely in writing this book.

Our first stop was in Honolulu at 0630 hours to refuel. I snapped two photos in the pre-dawn darkness of the plane before re-boarding on our way to Okinawa, a flight of nearly 10 hours. Again refueling, we began the final leg of our flight. At 1600 (4:00pm) on November 1, 1969, our plane touched down at Ben Hoa airfield, our flight's ultimate destination. According to a journal note, my stomach was grateful after having been quite queasy near the end of our trip. As we disembarked down the movable stairs, the reality of where I was quickly set in. The heat and humidity were just oppressive; I struggled to catch my breath and streams of sweat immediately trickled down my face. This would be my environment for the next year! Already I longed for the cool fall weather that I had left behind in the Midwest.

An Army bus, the shade of green that would become all too familiar in the color palette of the war, was waiting to shuttle us to nearby Long Binh where we were processed in and, at last, given time for a much-needed shower. In the holding area, there were no separate latrines for women. One of the chaplains who was also spending a couple days waiting for his final orders, stepped forward to assist in the dilemma by clearing out all the men periodically. The women would then take their turn. Our United States currency was exchanged for military issued MPCs—military payment certificates—our purchasing power during our stay in Vietnam. It reminded me of Monopoly money! Finally, we were outfitted with fatigues—solid Army green, no camouflage, made of heavy cotton. They were adjustable with two sets of buttons. I made sure that I started with the tightest button setting, as I doubted that I would be adding many pounds living on mess hall food in a war zone. Our boots were designed with green canvas sides and a steel plate in the sole to protect the foot should you step into a pungi pit. I had seen photos of such pits with their feces-smeared sharpened bamboo spikes disguised by layers of dried leaves and jungle overgrowth. I made a silent pledge to be extra careful if I found myself stomping through the jungle! During my time working in the emergency room, I would see the results of such missteps by some of the wounded GIs who were brought to the hospital. Very painful and deadly!

I assessed my new wardrobe selections—practical fabric, easy to mix and match though the color was not very flattering, lots of pockets for everything from tourniquets and clamps to pens and tissues. One thing was for sure, I made the right decision to leave at home the long underwear, wool skirt and long-sleeved shirt that I was issued at Ft. Sam. The temperature would never dip low enough to require those pieces.

When you take your first malaria preventative, you start a daily routine that continues throughout your time in Vietnam. From pigmenting your skin with a persimmon hue to punctuating your sleep with outrageous, Technicolor dreams, malaria pills may have kept mosquitoes from infecting you with a dreaded disease, but they also could disrupt your life. While we may have wondered if they were worth the trouble, I quickly changed my mind after caring for my first patient who had contracted malaria. Fever, chills, and drenching sweats—the disease is exhausting. I vowed early on to faithfully take my med each day.

My first full day behind me, I drifted off to sleep on a narrow bed with a metal frame and pancake thin mattress. In the morning we would get our duty assignment for the next year. I could not even hope and pray for a specific hospital because I had no clue what to pray for!

The next morning, as I stared at the sheet of paper in front of me, I did notice that the hospital, to which my former roommate at Ft. Dix had been assigned months earlier, was on the list—the 91st Evacuation Hospital in Chu Lai. I would at least know someone there when I arrived. In the two short days that I had been in country, I spent time with one of the other newly arrived nurses and we both decided to request Chu Lai. I was feeling a bit more comforted knowing that I would have two friends with me. Of course, as is typical of the Army, our requests were not guaranteed. I was, in fact, assigned to the 91st; my new friend was sent to the 93rd in Quang Tri in northern I Corp. She later told me that they were close enough to the DMZ that they could see the North Vietnamese women hanging out their laundry on Monday morning!

The next three days were filled with bits of orientation, time at the Officers' Club and several bus trips to the Ben Hoa airport and back, hoping to get on a flight north to I Corp. The military operation in Vietnam was divided into four "corps" or areas. Ben Hoa was in the south in IV Corp; Chu Lai was in the north in I Corp. Finally, on our fifth day in country, we were awakened and bussed to the airport at 0115 (1:15am). This time the plane was ready and we lifted off in the dark of night on a C-130, stopping in Qui Nhon, eventually landing in DaNang. There were only two nurses on the flight so we were invited to sit in the cockpit with the pilot and co-pilot. I took the engineer's seat and, wearing headphones, was able to follow our flight path. Forty years hence, that is hardly imaginable.

Descending onto the damp tarmac, I was given some news that was most unwelcome. Both my trunk and my duffle bag were not on the flight. Here I was, in the middle of a war, without so much as a toothbrush. I could feel the hot tears welling up in my tired eyes.

The two of us nurses were met by an ambulance which escorted us to another facility, the 67th Med group. It was at this point that my friend boarded a separate chopper for Quang Tri. I was truly on my own! Waiting to complete the final leg of this arduous journey was my helicopter, a HUEY, which lifted me up and then plopped me down at my home for the next year—the 91st Evacuation Hospital in Chu Lai, South Vietnam.

WELCOME TO CHU LAI

As I exited the chopper, remembering to keep my head down to prevent a serious head injury from the rotor blades, I was met by a Humpty Dumpty shaped man smoking a large stogie and sporting a bald head above a bushy moustache. LTC Utterback was the chief nurse of the hospital, destroying any Florence Nightingale image I may have had about the top nurse. His greeting and welcome were heartfelt and I began feeling a bit less lonely. However, being without even the basic grooming essentials quickly reminded me that all was not yet as I had hoped. Much of the first day was spent crying and trying to track down my missing luggage. In the end, my belongings and I were reunited over the next two days. My journal comment... "very relieved!"

My second day included a tour of the entire hospital. In one sense, it was very much like any other medical facility with space for surgical patients, an operating room, emergency room, intensive care unit, and wards for medical patients. However, there was also a Vietnamese unit for injured civilians and a locked POW ward for captured enemy soldiers. There were also facilities to house the relatives of Vietnamese patients. Generally, after we had stabilized those individuals, they were transferred to one of the local Vietnamese hospitals. The patient and accompanying family members all piled onto a helicopter for the flight back home.

As to the remainder of my first week in country, my journal mentions a visit to the "combat center" for training. Honestly, the only training that I remember involved two items—a reefer and a cultural handbook entitled "A Pocket Guide to Vietnam." I recall a small group of us passing around a lit marijuana cigarette so that we would know what it looked like and how it smelled should we be offered one. We were warned to avoid the weed. How odd, I thought. Equally strange was the book that covered everything from Vietnamese army insignia to local customs to how to behave in public. You would have thought that we were just vacationing there for a couple of weeks. I still have the book, but used it very little. One statement listed under "Dos and Don'ts" in South Vietnam reads—"Don't give the impression the U.S. is running the war." Looking back, this is almost humorous! As to the smoking question, I never took up marijuana because its sweet smell made me queasy. The truth!

For my first three weeks at Chu Lai, I was assigned to share a room with another nurse who also was a newbie. Judy and I got along quite well, both trying to familiarize ourselves with our surroundings as well as meeting other nurses, doctors, and hospital staff. We found out quickly that, while time on duty was serious stuff, after hours offered a variety of opportunities for relaxing and trying to forget what we had dealt with just an hour before.

After three weeks, I was given my own room. Approximately 9x12 feet in size, three of the walls were solid wood, the fourth one being screen with wooden louvers. The screen kept out the bugs, mosquitoes and most rodents. It also allowed the sea breeze to waft through when the steamy tropical weather made sleeping difficult. During the months that the monsoon rains drenched everything, the wooden louvers over the screened wall saved the room from flooding. My humble home was smartly furnished with one single sized metal bed with a lumpy mattress that had seen better days. The only other piece of furniture, when I first arrived, was a tall metal cabinet in the usual shade of green. It held about 10 hangers and shelves for a month's worth of clothes, but I would be staying for a full year. The trunk that was finally located, with the addition of a piece of colorful fabric, became a nightstand and I purchased an oscillating fan from the person who had occupied the room prior to my arrival. The fan would be a necessity during the dry season when temperatures could rise above 120 degrees Fahrenheit. To accommodate wet clothes during the rainy season, I strung a short piece of rope across one corner of the room.

The PX (short for post exchange, like K-mart for the military) was our closest shopping venue, unless you left the compound and drove to a local Vietnamese village marketplace. However, if you wanted products available in the United States, the PX was your sole source. The challenge with shopping there was finding something that you wanted or needed WHEN you wanted or needed it. While there was usually an ample supply of "Beanie Weanies" and condoms, you might not find socks, soap, or shampoo. Cigarettes were always in demand, but occasionally filtered ones were nowhere in sight and you had to settle for Camels or Lucky Strikes, unfiltered. Those of us women who did smoke lit up a lot less when we had to pick bits of tobacco off our tongues. (I quit smoking over 35 years ago but still remember that nasty tobacco.) One item that there seemed to be no shortage of was men's pants hangers. I never understood the reasoning, as guys coming in from the bush surely were not anxious to hang up their muddy fatigue bottoms! From a realistic point of view, there was nowhere to hang them. They must have been a cheap purchase item!

One of the first items that I purchased at the PX was a pair of black lacquered vases with inlaid mother-of-pearl designs. Why? I must have really liked them. They definitely were not a necessity, but did add a touch of class to my meager furnishings. They still have a special place on our family room shelf.

In addition to stocked merchandise, one could order items from PACEX—a mail order catalog (Pacific Exchange). I ordered several larger items because of the high quality and low price. Our fine china dinnerware by Noritake was purchased and sent directly home via PACEX. The price for twelve place settings rimmed in gold with all the serving pieces—$96! It continues to grace our table on special occasions.

ON DUTY

My first assignment at the 91st was to one of the four medical wards. Located at the opposite end of the hospital from the emergency room, my patients included anyone who needed treatment for a malady not resultant from an injury. The list of ailments included malaria, hepatitis, jungle rot, intestinal worms, and parasites. Less common was the occasional non-war condition such as heart disease. I tended to a colonel who had had a heart attack and was on my ward until he was stable enough to be flown back to the States. He was pleased enough with my care to write a commendation for me. And yes, of course, I still have it!

While in the hospital, all the medical patients were required to wear regulation blue hospital outfits designed like operating room scrubs. If they were able, they made their own beds, were responsible for taking meds, even helped around the ward. Many played cards or read to pass the time. They loved being safe and dry. Having a bed to sleep in was a luxury, knowing that they were headed back to the bush as soon as the physician gave the OK. For many, this was a mini R&R. For others, especially the malaria sufferers, their stay was not as pleasant.

Malaria, caused by a microorganism carried by the Anopheles mosquito, was rampant in the marshy environment of Vietnam. Everyone serving there was given malaria prophylactic meds to take, but often the guys ran out. Some hated to take it because one often experienced very strange dreams and nightmares. Others hated the orangish tint that it gave their skin. These concerns paled in comparison to the symptoms that those who contracted the disease had to face. Raging fevers alternating with teeth-rattling chills, headaches, and profuse sweating continued for several days. The disease also remains dormant in the body for years to come. I have read accounts that some guys chose not to take the malaria med in order to contract the disease, sending them to a hospital for a few weeks to get a break from the jungle. I cannot confirm that that was not the case, but I doubt there were many who made that decision.

Contaminated water and/or food presented a variety of nasty possibilities. Hepatitis, intestinal parasites or worms, and plain old food poisoning all meant a trip to the hospital when the soldier came out of the bush.

Nausea and diarrhea accompanied most of these illnesses and the hospital afforded a more bathroom-friendly environment than the jungle. Antibiotics and rest were the treatments of choice for these maladies.

Combat boots were ideal for hiking through swampy areas and rough terrain, but, when they got wet, it took days for them to dry out. Wet feet in wet boots in wet marshes led to large open sores on the feet and lower legs. Throw in a few leeches that were lurking in the murky waters and you have the perfect recipe for jungle rot. Walking became extremely painful and could lead to serious vascular infection. After a few days in the hospital, allowing the sores to dry up in the open air along with 10 days of antibiotics and no walking, the legs healed and the soldier generally returned to his unit—with dry boots and socks. Many would return for repeat treatment, as the insufferable conditions remained unchanged.

I served on the medical wards from November through February 1970. Our workweek consisted of twelve-hour shifts (7 to 7) six days a week. We were given a 3-hour break at specific times during the day shift if it was possible to "get away." Generally, while I was on the medical wards, I was able to make use of that break time. Later, when I moved to the Emergency Room, the workload often prevented anyone from leaving for even a brief period.

After I had spent three months on the medical wards, the chief nurse offered me the chance to move to the emergency room (R&E—receiving and emergency). Without hesitation, I accepted the opportunity. The thought of being as close to the action as I could really appealed to me. I had had excellent training in my nursing school, spent time nursing stateside, and acclimated to life in a war zone. I felt ready to tackle what I considered the most intensive of the nursing specialties, especially in a combat theater. The date was 20 February 1970, eight days before my twenty-third birthday.

Looking back on that day, I realize that no one can truly be prepared for the type of trauma nursing that I would experience over the next eight months. On my second day in R&E, a young man was brought in on a stretcher missing both legs. I had never seen a bilateral amputee before. Dried blood was caked to his fatigues, hands, face, and IV bottle lying next to him on the litter. The medic in the field had bandaged his stumps, started the fluids and given him morphine; it was up to us to take it from there. The standard procedure was to cut off all his clothes so we could thoroughly assess the extent of his injuries. Modesty took a backseat to saving a life. In many cases, time was of the essence. After making all the necessary adjustments and notes, he was covered with a sheet and whisked into pre-op on his way to surgery. He was 19. When I got off duty, a bunch of us celebrated my birthday with a cake sent by my mom. That evening I was blowing out birthday candles; the next morning, my patient was waking up to a new life, without legs.

Over the ensuing months, I made several journal entries about the type of day I was having, regarding patients and wounds. Entries such as: "Insane day with 20+ GIs—burns frag wds, triple amp, DOA and KIA. Absolutely makes me sick!" or "Mas cal (mass casualties) at 1815. 52 pts all together, 16 at 11:00" filled the pages of my journal. (Translation—burns, fragmentation wounds, triple amputee, dead on arrival and killed in action. 52 patients) Another day I wrote: "Very busy past 3 days; no breaks. Corpsman shot in barracks."

Vietnamese civilians were not immune to the ravages of war either. According to some records, as many as 164,000 Vietnamese civilians were killed during the war. Age, gender, occupation—none of these mattered to the soldiers from the North. When there was reason to suspect that a village was sheltering U.S. friendly ARVN soldiers (Army of the Republic of Vietnam), the enemy needed no further cause to attack. Sometimes a specific family or group would be targeted. On occasion an entire community was hit. In May 1970, we suffered a "mas cal." Ninety-nine wounded Vietnamese civilians passed through our Emergency Room in less than 24 hours!

On another occasion, a wounded GI presented a more personal connection for me. A lieutenant whom I had met when I first arrived in country was carried in on a litter. I was not attending to him, but as I cared for the young man on the litter next to him I instantly recognized his southern drawl. He was from Georgia and was serving with an artillery unit not far from the hospital. His body was peppered with shrapnel and covered with dried blood, but he was awake and talking, generally a positive sign. As they wheeled him into surgery, the nurse who had been with him said that he would probably lose both of his legs due to the circulatory damage. That was the only time that I broke down and had to leave the ER to compose myself. This person was someone that I knew and that made the hurt even deeper. Later in the recovery room, he told me that he pleaded with the surgeon to not amputate his legs. They granted his wish though not offering him much hope about his rehabilitation possibilities. He was quickly evacuated to Tokyo and then back to the United States. As a postscript to the story, I visited him stateside when I returned. He was recovering in the hospital at Ft. Benning and still had his legs though they were weak and facing years of physical therapy. He bravely walked with two canes with much determination. I think of him from time to time, playing the harmonica and charming the nurses with his silky, soft voice. I find myself wondering if those legs survived to carry him down life's road.

WORKING NIGHTS

We worked twelve hour shifts during my time at the 91st—7 am to 7 pm or the reverse. While working the night shift messed with one's interior clock, I loved the quiet that generally descended upon those hours of the day. The fighting often slowed at night, casual visits for less serious issues dropped off at night and auxiliary personnel (lab, x-ray, etc) were only available as an on-call basis. I do remember one particular young kid who had made a visit to the local village brothel and came in for a shot of penicillin. He was leery about "dropping his drawers" to get the shot in his backside. Thinking quickly on my feet, I replied, "If you had not dropped them earlier this evening, you would not be having to do it now!" It was one of the lighter moments in the emergency room.

Another reason that there was less activity on the night shift was because of the danger posed to helicopters attempting to rescue injured soldiers in the dark. Under cover of darkness, the most effective means of locating someone was with the use of flares. While the bright glow of a flare alerted the rescue chopper, it also told the enemy where you were located. Not good! Much of Vietnam was covered with a thick canopy of foliage hindering the pilot's view from the air of wounded below. Even Agent Orange could not defoliate all of the vegetation.

Just as everyone feels a bit uncomfortable in new surroundings at night, so too were we keenly aware of things that would "go bump in the night." Most sapper attacks took place after sunset. While such attacks were not daily events, the ones that I recall all occurred after it was dark. They were carried out by an elite troop of NVA (North Vietnamese Army), or VC (Viet Cong) who were trained in perimeter infiltration. Generally working alone, these individuals, armed with wire cutters and knives, would snip the barbed wire surrounding a compound such as the hospital, low crawling their way into the protected area. These were akin to suicide missions because the intruder was generally killed. The goal was to get to him (or her) before he killed one of us. Despite guards and fences, one was always on alert, especially at night.

Sometimes, staying awake was the biggest challenge when working the 7 pm to 7 am shift. We tried to keep ourselves occupied with conversation, trips to the mess hall for midnight snacks and, at the 91st, with Scrabble. We would balance the game board on a metal trashcan and try to outspell each other. There was no Scrabble dictionary to consult when we questioned an unfamiliar word. We just took a vote to allow or reject the entry. Generally, there was only one nurse on duty at night, but there were always at least two corpsmen, just enough players for the game. If casualties arrived, we simply set the game aside, took care of the new arrivals, and resumed the game when quiet returned to the ER.

BREAK TIME

One of the highlights of our workday was the "free time" that we were allowed if time permitted. At our hospital, there were designated blocks of time during the day when we could get away from the wards and do whatever we pleased. Reading, journaling, working on our tans at the beach, taking the boat out for a bit of water-skiing—all were possibilities for break time! Since most of the wards, including the ER, were not air-conditioned, time on the beach or water-skiing was a blessing. Depending on the time of day, weather, sea conditions, and allotted time, most of us either descended the wooden steps to our postage stamp sized beach for some rays, or met at the tiny boat launch for a few runs of water skiing. I never knew where the boat and skis had come from, but I spent many hours enjoying the thrill of gliding across the waters of the South China Sea. Was it dangerous? Perhaps so. We did adhere to the local belief that sharks made appearances after 1:00 p.m. and we respected their space, keeping out of the water in the afternoon. Of course, if the hospital had taken rocket fire, we would have been vulnerable. I suppose we figured that the odds of a rocket actually hitting our tiny boat were pretty slim. After all, there were many more strategic sights for the enemy to target than a couple of water skiers on break! If down time was a matter of just a few minutes, you could catch some ZZZs lying on a litter. I always felt however, that, when possible, it was better to physically remove myself from the hospital to more deeply relax and collect my thoughts.

The one activity that was discouraged during break time was drinking alcohol. Knowing that you were due back when your break was finished was not conducive to getting that relaxed. The most treasured breaks were either the first or last break—7:00 to 10:00 a.m. meant that you could sleep in a bit; 4:00-7:00 p.m. offered the promise of getting off early, unless the VC planned an attack in the late afternoon.

Having time off in the middle of the day also provided an opportunity to shop at the PX, wash clothes, write letters or spend time with friends away from the blood and pain of war. There was always music playing in someone's room or hootch to remind you of home. Sometimes the best use of free time was simply a nap—generally well-deserved! However the time was spent, having it taken away was greeted with much distain and grumbling. In my journal, I noted on April 9, "Breaks taken away. Everyone furious!" Generally this happened when there was an anticipation of a large number of incoming wounded. Sitting around and waiting for patients was never a pleasant experience.

OFF DUTY

There were many other memorable and challenging times in the emergency room, but we did find relief, if only temporarily, from the stress of our work. Our down time was very important. There was always a gathering, in someone's hootch or room, at the Officers' Club, or down on our tiny beach. Alcohol, music, laughter, and lively conversation took our minds off the day's work. I have often said that we worked very hard and played very hard.

Whether strumming my guitar, water-skiing, journaling, or just resting, that time away from torment and death gave balance to my days and helped restore my sanity, allowing me to face a new round of casualties the next day. Water-skiing was very freeing; the sea refreshed your spirit. "Red tide"algae and sharks were always of concern, but the risks were worth the euphoric pleasure. On occasion, we would toss the towrope to a Vietnamese fisherman sitting in his LRB (little round boat) in the bay and give him a ride. He would bounce along behind our powerboat, laughing with each jump of a wave. At the finish, he would give us a thumbs-up sign and proclaim "number 1" which meant "the best." Anything that was terrible was "number 10"; digits in between were not usually expressed. It was either very good or very bad!

I often found myself singing the latest folk music, not just on the beach, but at the Officer's Club, in my room, most anywhere. I had not taken my guitar to Vietnam, but asked a doctor to purchase one for me while he was on R&R in Tokyo. It is the same guitar that I have played for the last forty-five years. Today, many of the songs of that era instantly transport me back to Chu Lai—"Proud Mary," "Leaving on a Jet Plane," "Bridge Over Troubled Waters," "Both Sides Now."

We occasionally had dances at the Officer's Club. A group of GIs who were musicians before entering the

Army were assigned to form a band and take their music to guys in the field. They also loved to jam at the O Club and we were thrilled when they did. They even let me sing along as well as accompany them on an occasional foray to an LZ (landing zone). I remember one particular trip when we boarded a Chinook with all the instruments, including a drum set. We took off with the floor of the helicopter open because we were toting a large cargo load in a net under the belly of the chopper. I have great photos of the terrain below us showing bomb craters, rice paddies, and water buffalo. I can't recall if we were strapped in, but luckily no one fell out!

The GIs at the LZ were very excited, not just to hear the band, but also to catch a glimpse of an American woman. During the Vietnam War, there were no women in direct combat. I must admit that I got plenty of attention that day, even attired in dusty fatigues with sand embedded in my wind blown hair! I also gained a deeper appreciation for the conditions that the grunts endured. The LZ was a heavenly oasis, a "vacation" from the bush. Yet, when I was there during the dry season, APC's, large armored personnel carriers, created red clouds of eye-stinging dust as they moved about. The only structures scattered throughout were several large tents where they served real food, rather than C-rations, and fresh water. There were enclosed latrines so no one had to dig a hole to do their thing. I quickly realized how nice we had it living on the hospital compound with a mess hall, roof over our heads and real showers—most of the time. It was no wonder that so many GIs turned to alcohol or drugs to mask their daily travails.

On rare occasions, we escaped from the realities of the war with an evening getaway to an American restaurant called the "Jaded Duck." Just a few minutes off post, its tiny dining area had perhaps 10 tables with no serious ambiance, but it was "away" from the hospital. We dressed in civvies—real clothes, not fatigues. I don't recall that the food was outstanding, but it was a welcome change from day to day Army grub. The best part about "the Duck" was that they had a large screen and showed current movies. This was long before video tapes; they had big reels of film like movie theaters. I remember seeing "Bob and Carol and Ted and Alice" there while sipping glasses of Mateus wine. Such a treat!

STAYING IN TOUCH

I often think of how different my experience would have felt had I been able to communicate with family back home via email or Skype like the soldiers have done in recent conflicts from foreign combat regions. Our first, and slowest, option in 1969, was the U.S. mail. Generally, it took one to two weeks to get a letter home or to receive one from the States. At least the postage was free if you had an APO address. We used special airmail stationery that was so thin that, should you try to write on both sides of a sheet, it would bleed through, making it a challenge to decipher the wording. The nearly transparent stationery did keep the weight of mailbags to a minimum. Less poundage, more room for cargo and troops.

My favorite means of letting my parents know what was happening in my world was to record messages on a tiny recorder. I purchased one shortly after my arrival along with blank reel-to-reel tapes. The 2" reels were then placed in special plastic mailing containers and sent back to the States. They afforded the convenience of rambling on for about thirty minutes. With the built-in microphone, I recorded carefully selected tidbits of my day to share with my loved ones. Generally, I steered clear of body counts and graphic descriptions and concentrated on what I was up to in my spare time, how many patients I had, why they were in the hospital, etc. Of course, not everything that I did while off duty was appropriate for sharing with my parents and younger siblings.

The details, voiced on those tapes to my family, have remained a secret. Several years ago, when I started wondering what exactly I did say to my parents, I unearthed the box that had held those bits of information about life in a wartime hospital. There they were, a couple dozen reels of memories just waiting to be replayed. Alas, when I affixed the first tape to the aging recorder, all I could hear was music. I tried a second reel and then a third. Just more music. My mother, frugal woman that she was, allowed my young brother to record over the tapes with his favorite music. Even a professional audio/video company could not undo the music. How I wish I had those tapes to refer to today.

It was possible to phone home though we did not do that very often. One could use the MARS line, which stands for Military Amateur Radio System. It was a bit confusing because you had to say "over" when you finished speaking in order for the line to become available to the person on the other end. My mother got nervous and would say "over" first which sent the line right back to me! She did finally get the hang of it and it helped if I called her early in the day and not late at night. The time difference was twelve hours to my home in the Midwest. My dad decided that it was easier to just let mom talk and wait for her report!

The last option was to use a phone housed in the Red Cross office. It was a real phone without any confusing operations. It was primarily reserved for emergencies or very special occasions. It also was only available for use at certain times of the day.

Care packages from home brought keeping in touch to a much higher level. It was impossible to keep the arrival of a box at mail call a secret, especially if it contained food. Cookies, homemade were the best, candy that did not melt in the jungle heat, or large jars of peanut butter were all cause for a celebration. My mother had taken up the hobby of cake decorating shortly before I left the States. For my birthday, she carefully created a beautiful confection with blue and white icing, packing it within many layers of waxed paper and plastic wrap inside two cardboard boxes for stability. Upon opening the box, the cake, having endured its three-week journey from Illinois to Chu Lai, was a distorted mass of cake and frosting. After imagining what it once looked like, we set upon the former work of art with spoons, forks and fingers until the last crumb was consumed. Appearance aside, it was one of my most memorable birthday cakes!

The only newspaper to keep us up to date on the latest happenings in the rest of the world was the military paper the "Stars and Stripes." Because it was a government publication, we often sensed that it did not openly present both sides of issues, especially when it came to reporting on the war and the casualty counts. There was no Internet or television to offer an opposing point of view. We did know, from letters that we received from our families, that back in the States the "facts" of the war were not completely truthful. The body counts reported in the US media indicated that the U.S. forces were losing far fewer lives than we were recording.

VISITORS FROM "THE WORLD"

While a stay in Vietnam was not on the agenda of most travelers in 1969, we did occasionally welcome visitors. Of course, there were the less-than-exciting "top brass" officers that wandered through the wards to check on the wounded, hand out Purple Hearts and try to lift the morale of the soldiers. Many of the men considered these efforts merely photo ops for the news photographers who were seeking a picture for the front page of their newspapers. "General So-and-So showing support for our fighting men in Vietnam." Even the conferring of Purple Hearts or Bronze Stars was met with a "so what" attitude by some of the wounded. One soldier proclaimed that they handed medals out like candy. "Everybody gets one!" When a young otherwise healthy man has lost a leg or arm, can a small piece of metal on a ribbon make up for that loss?

I actually have a Purple Heart, given to me by a returned wounded soldier who I cared for at Ft. Dix, before I left for Vietnam. I had just gotten my orders and was sharing that information with some of my patients. One young man, with a slowly healing leg wound that had gotten infected, opened his bedside stand and handed me a navy colored leather box. I opened it and found a Purple Heart resting on the velvet interior. "Take it!" he stated emphatically. "If you are going to Nam to take care of wounded guys, you deserve it!" Despite numerous protests from me, he refused to take it back. When I share my Vietnam experiences with students, I show them the medal and make it clearly understood that it was a gift, not an award for bravery. I am grateful for being able to share it with others, but often wonder if the now aging vet ever regrets parting with his medal.

Personally, I am very honored to have been given recognition for my combat service by a fellow soldier because the hierarchy of the Army chose not to acknowledge the contributions of most nurses who served. I do not personally know of one nurse who was awarded a bronze star, except for Sharon Lane who died in a rocket attack at the hospital. Perhaps women's contributions to the war effort in country weren't given fair consideration because of the popular perception of women as selfless caregivers whose contributions in that area were less deserving of recognition. In a way, we are still waiting for our "welcome home."

The arrival of other visitors was far more exciting. The USO had traveling shows that would visit some of the hospitals and compounds. Some were dance troups, which always pleased the men. On other occasions, popular musical artists and ensembles stopped by. I particularly enjoyed the New Christy Minstrels who performed shortly after I arrived at the hospital. Their folk style music was my favorite and I was grateful for the opportunity to sing along on a couple pieces. Rummaging through some relics of my past, I found a pen and ink drawing on a piece of brown paper sack drawn by Travis, a member of the group. Ah, the things I have saved!

When it came to memorable entertainers, however, no one created more excitement than Bob Hope with his cadre of gorgeous women and well-known celebrities. Because there was a large outdoor amphitheater located on the Americal Division compound, just down the hill from our hospital, it was a perfect setting for him. The troops started gathering early the morning of the show. I have no idea how it was decided who could attend, but every inch of the long bench seats was covered as the troops crowded in closely. We wheeled patients down on gurneys if their docs gave their approval. Wheelchair bound patients in the classic blue pajamas and robes were given space down front. Some of the able-bodied even climbed up the light poles scattered around the area.

Bob appeared with his trademark prop, a "wood" golf club, dishing out one-liners to the delight of everyone. His jokes were always specifically directed to the individual location in country. He was quite familiar with the different bases having done his Christmas tours annually since WWII. In 1969, when I was lucky enough to be in the audience, his entourage included astronaut Neil Armstrong, actress and singer Connie Stevens, Miss World and the Golddiggers—a group of tall, statuesque dancers who were performers on the Dean Martin show. The women were all attired in long, shapely, sequined gowns, evoking a chorus of wolf whistles and applause. Now THAT was what improved troop morale! That December day, as we laughed, clapped and sang along, the skies suddenly opened up, drenching all of us in monsoon rains. No one moved. As the show ended, our faces were wet with a combination of rain and tears while we joined our voices together in "Silent Night." I relive that memory each time I hear that most loved classic.

Occasionally, someone would receive unexpected visitors—a friend from another unit who managed to find some reason to be near an old buddy, or an experience that I had when an old boyfriend showed up. That, however, is a long story that I will save for a later chapter.

SPIRITUALITY

There is an old expression that says, "There are no atheists in fox holes." What that really points out is the fact that when one finds oneself in difficult circumstances, prayer seems to be the direction to go. It is easy to endeavor to make a pact with the Lord. "If you get me out of this alive I will do such and such." It was my experience that while many of us called on the Lord for help, that plea was often splattered with plenty of swearing just for extra emphasis. Most of the units had chaplains assigned to them and occasionally there were organized services, but those were few and far between. There was a chapel on our hospital compound and we had a Catholic chaplain for a period of time. He would offer Mass on Sunday, which I tried to attend. Chaplains of other denominations were located in the general area for those who wanted to attend particular services. However, for the guys out in the bush, organized worship was not the usual practice. Most often the chaplain was the one who visited the wounded and fallen GIs in the field. Their job was surely a challenging one, whether giving the Last Rites, hearing a troubled confession, or just listening and comforting.

WAR IS NOT A RAMBO FLICK

The moment I disembarked from the plane in Long Binh, I discovered that the reality of war was quite different from what was portrayed on the movie screen. To begin with, most of the GIs were thin, quiet, freckle-faced teenagers. They were not gym-hardened musclemen with huge biceps, terrific tans, and shiny greased bodies. While certain elite units, who trained for many months, were of superior strength, the average draftee was not. Basic training offered a few weeks of practice crawling under barbwire and climbing over fences carrying as much as 40 pounds of weapons and rounds of ammunition. Unless the soldier had been in great shape from high school sports, he was probably not prepared for the strength and endurance that he would need to do battle. When basic training ended, many guys were thinner, worn out and ready for leave. They missed their mother's home cooking, a good hot bath or shower, and people who weren't shouting orders at them all day. Most hoped for a stateside assignment, though many knew they eventually would be headed to Vietnam.

Other recruits were professional—docs, lawyers, administrators. Though some signed up because they knew they would be drafted, they did not fit the Rambo image either. Many were not trained for the harsh realities of war. Often they found themselves doing hands-on learning, the work it out-as-you-go method. Most of the doctors were clearly dealing with injuries, wounds, and diseases that they had never dealt with in the past. Too frequently, situations were truly life-and-death scenarios. Unless their medical training took place in a large, perhaps inner-city hospital, the type of trauma experienced in Vietnam was unlike anything else. Considering their situations, many of them proved to be excellent practitioners. Battlefield medicine is unique. Unlike in the movies, the blood was real, the pain intense, and not all the good guys walked away heroes in one piece.

UNDER FIRE

According to my journal, the first rocket attack that I experienced, targeting our hospital, was on January 25th, two and a half months after I arrived. If the compound received any advanced notice of an impending attack, a siren would sound. The protocol was to grab one's steel pot (helmet) and flak jacket, running to the nearest bunker for protection. Bunkers came in lots of different designs with one purpose in mind—to offer some protection in a rocket attack. Generally they were constructed of large metal culverts piled high with sandbags. There was one directly outside my door. I suppose that it was considered a luxury model as it came with two long benches inside. Unfortunately, other things were inside as well, rats! The first person in had the privilege of shooing out the rats.

Your steel pot and flak jacket were generally in your room, which meant that, if you were on duty when the sirens blasted the compound, there was no time to run to your room to get them. In that a case, you and your patients were to crawl under the beds for protection. Remembering that Sharon Lane had been killed during a rocket attack just a few months earlier brought the realization that a hospital bed might not afford sufficient protection during such an attack. But it was the best one could do. Such events frequently led to that "bargaining with the Lord."

When the siren blew a second time, it was an all-clear signal for us to crawl out of the bunkers or out from under the beds. I always wondered how confident the person making that determination could be. Surely the Viet Cong did not give our side a call to say that they were all finished attacking for the day! Perhaps it was determined by the lack of that whistling sound as the rockets sailed overhead and splashed into the South China Sea. While the quiet signaled an end to the rockets, in a way, that splash was a welcome sound for we knew they had missed their target—us!

Over the forty-five plus years since my tour, I have

read accounts by other nurses who were stationed at the 91st for part of the time that I was there. One spoke of frequent rocket attacks and fearing for her life on a weekly basis. With the passage of time, our memories fade but I do not remember attacks coming that often. For the Viet Cong, holidays were reasons for celebration. Tet (the Vietnamese New Year), the spring equinox, the start of winter—all came with a promise of attacks. The enemy chose to mark the occasion by propelling mortar rounds at U.S. and South Vietnamese compounds.

There certainly were enough attacks to keep us all on edge even if they didn't occur on a weekly basis. One thing we knew for sure, when we were under attack, the troops located near the hospital compound were also under attack. There would be casualties and we would soon start receiving them.

PHOTOGRAPHS

SOUTH VIETNAM

Map of South Vietnam with military units and their locations

48

Taken on day four after I arrived in Long Binh waiting for a flight to Chu Lai

The band called Chiefs of Staff loading up a Chinook in Chu Lai for visit to LZ

Bob Hope show at the Americal division amphitheater in Chu Lai

Ward 5 at 91st Evac housed medical patients—malaria, hepatitis, intestinal parasites, boot jungle rot. One heart attack victim. I worked there from November 1969 to February 1970.

Vietnamese boy with shrapnel wound to eye. His eyeball was
spared and he had plastic surgery to rebuild his eyelid.

Empty R&E (emergency room) March to October 1970

R&E in action

The room that I first shared for three weeks with a roommate

BOQ where I lived by myself for the rest of the year—lower left,
orange door

Taken at the LZ when I performed with the band.
Just being goofy!

91st Evacuation Hospital taken from a LOCH (light observation chopper). I took this photo while flying with a friend. The Americal Division amphitheater is in the background.

View of the beach at the 91st taken from the officers club.

Vietnamese fisherman in LRB (little round boat)

Hootches—accommodations for hospital staff officers

Ready to go water-skiing

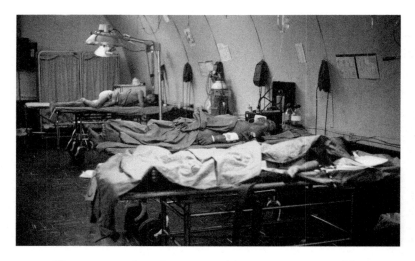

Vietnamese patients in pre-op waiting to go to surgery. The patient in the background is having shrapnel removed under local anesthesia.

Vietnamese patients, having been stabilized, are returned to the local Vietnamese hospital via Huey helicopter.

The sun setting over the mountains behind South China Sea. Laundry drying near BOQ

Refreshment stand along Highway One on the road to Hue. This photo was taken the weekend of our drive from Danang to Hue. Cans and bottles at such locations were often booby-trapped.

The view from the plane window of Hong Kong upon arrival for R&R Aug 1970

An orphaned Montagnard girl. She was eventually adopted by an Army nurse.

Rocket attack hitting oil storage tank on beach south of hospital

My final day in Vietnam. 91st Evac Hospital in background

Catching up with two other nurses (Barb and Rosie) from the 91st
Evac at the dedication of the Vietnam Women's Memorial, Washington DC, November 1993

62

The Wall, Washington DC. Sharon Lane's name, one of 8 women listed. Sharon was on duty when a rocket hit the hospital four months before my arrival there.

Vietnam Women's Memorial in Washington DC

Visiting the cockpit of a 747 on my first return trip to Vietnam, November 1994—definitely a thing of the past.

Enjoying a BaBaBa beer at the rooftop bar of the Rex Hotel in Saigon, a ritual I would enjoy at the the start of each visit.

A final look inside the Maison Centrale prison (Hanoi Hilton) in 1996, which housed POWs including John McCain. The Prison was being demolished to make room for a high-rise hotel. Part of the building was retained and became a museum.

Exiting the infamous tunnels of Cu Chi, outside of Saigon.

With friend Mary Starr on China Beach near Da Nang, January 1996.

The original gate to the Chu Lai complex. Photo taken on second
return trip, January 1996. The hospital and remaining buildings of
the entire compound had been demolished.

Storage bunkers remaining from the war near Da Nang,
October 2013.

Returning to Cu Chi 20 years later October 2013

With my husband in front of Ho Chi Minh's tomb in Hanoi, October 2013. It was Halloween, thus the skeleton earrings!

A Vietnamese woman shopping at the floating market in Delta,
October 2014

Returning to China beach, 2014

Cyclo ride in the rain in Hue 2014

With Chase Davis, a student from College of the Ozarks, near Chu Lai, soon to be the site of a new airport, October 2014

2014 view of fishing village, Lan Co, from Hai Van Pass. This photo is nearly identical to one taken in 1970. This is one of my favorite views in the entire country!

Checking out a C-130 at War Museum in Khe Sanh

Inside Hanoi Hilton museum, replica of cell, Oct 2014

Former POW Bill Bailey explains aspects of his confinement during the war to students from the College of the Ozarks in 2014.

Leaving after my fourth visit to the Hanoi Hilton in September 2014

74

INVISIBLE WOUNDS

The real tragedy of any war is that not all wounds present themselves to even the most observant medical personnel. There are weapons that can destroy the very soul of the victim, leaving behind little evidence of having crippled a soldier. I am referring to shell shock, foxhole fear, post-traumatic stress disorder (PTSD). Each generation gave it a different title but the symptoms are the same and the pain just as deep now as it was in previous wars. Whether the engagement is called a war, conflict or intervention, the stress of combat cannot be denied.

Contributing factors have been cited as age, lack of preparation, immaturity, and unrealistic expectations. Add to these the realization that the sole purpose of combat is to overtake the enemy by whatever means at your disposal. Talk about being over-stressed!

Looking more closely at the above factors, think of where you were at age nineteen or twenty. In college, working for a local business, taking trade classes. Enter the military, which shaves your head, fits you for stiff green fatigues and decrees what you can and cannot do. Just as you were enjoying the freedom of being out of your parents' house, you are back to a serious schedule and being told what to do and when. Then you are given 6-8 weeks of training on weapons, bandaging, low crawling under barbed wire, and field stripping a cigarette filter. At home the only decisions that were yours alone were what to wear and eat, who to hang out with, and where your future would take you. Then your government comes calling in a manila envelope and your world is turned upside down.

For many young soldiers who served in Vietnam, the life-style of the military was in itself like moving to a foreign country. It involved communal living, sharing everything with little privacy, being told where and when to be in a less than friendly voice, and tolerating personalities very different from yours. Suddenly you have lost all control and must answer to your platoon leader or suffer the consequences. At the same time, you are expected to make decisions that might result in the wounding or even death of others. Add to this stress-filled atmosphere, the casualties that can happen the first time that you are caught in an ambush. Your buddy, crouching next to you is hit, blood spurting from his muddied leg evoking cries of pain. He calls out for his mother or girlfriend. He begs you to not let him die. You hadn't really deeply considered that this would happen. Real blood, real tears, real cries of "Help me!"

Another challenge for the U.S. soldier in Vietnam was how to distinguish the enemy from friendly troops, particularly the Viet Cong, who were often attired in black silk "pajamas," the loose fitting two piece outfits that were the everyday clothing of many Vietnamese civilians. Unlike previous wars, where the opposing forces could be easily distinguished by their uniforms and insignia, this was not the case in Vietnam. Weathered faces, diminutive stature, common language, and conical hats were identical for both sides.

Imagine wandering in the razor-sharp elephant grass for days, perhaps not having much to eat or drink, surviving on only a few hours of restless sleep as the monsoon rains drench even your underwear (if you own any) when you suddenly detect a rustling in the reeds. Not knowing who or what is responsible for the sound, you must make a choice to advance, shoot, or just lay low, hoping that the decision will not cost you your life or the lives of your fellow soldiers. Even after confronting the mystery intruder, he appears to be a local farmer. But is he also a VC sympathizer? Does he have children who are spreading propaganda among the villagers? Are the VC paying him for information about the locations or movements of troops? Does he become a sniper under the cover of night, snipping the barbed wire around a hospital, crawling on his belly and shooting an unexpected passerby?

Often the invisible trauma of PTSD takes much longer to present itself and, unlike a physical injury that visibly heals, psychological wounds may never completely resolve. I recently heard of a former Army nurse who had a flashback, her first in 30 years! What was it that caused her mind to bring up this bad episode after all these years? Perhaps it was a smell or the mention of a place. Maybe the tone of a stranger's voice or a loud bang in the distance that suddenly put her back in another place and time.

Did I return with PTSD? Clearly my life was greatly affected by the experience of spending a year in a war zone. When I returned from Vietnam, little things troubled me—loud noises, the whop-whop of a helicopter flying overhead, a song, maybe a news report. I did have dreams, I suppose that they could be called nightmares, but not the type that cause one to act out or attack one's sleeping companion. I do not recall waking up in a cold sweat or screaming out that I was being hunted down or running for my life. The one personality trait that I found to be most exacerbated by my war experience was my inability to control my tears. As a child, I frequently would burst into tears if I was excluded from an activity that I really wanted to be part of. My mother often accused me of being overly dramatic. It was just my persona. Tell me "no" and the tears came easily. However, after Vietnam, the weepy tendency became even more pronounced. Just the sight of an injured person or animal was enough to set me off. If I called a business for assistance and was told that they could not help me, I would feel my face turn red and the wetness well up in my eyes. Clearly, while trying to show a tough exterior, my damp eyes gave me away. I simply seemed to be more sensitive to everyday disappointments. It was not a quality that I have been proud of.

Along similar lines, I have no desire to read books

or watch movies that are gut wrenching. Perhaps I saw enough pain and destruction during the war; I just don't want to endure more sadness. I can get plenty of that on the evening news; I do not need to take in more violence, regardless of how "well made" the film is. I have watched a few movies where the theme of the story was the Vietnam War, such as *Born On The Fourth of July* and *Platoon*. *Platoon* was the first that I saw and I chose to go by myself in the middle of the afternoon, a rare happening for me. I was not certain how it would affect me and did not want to embarrass myself in front of even my husband. I actually just sat numbly in my seat not really able to express any emotion. Perhaps the fact that I knew it was fiction, masked my feelings.

The psychological effects of spending time under the influence of war clearly vary from one individual to another. My challenges are very minor compared to some who are yet haunted by overwhelming nightmares prohibiting a decent night's sleep or flashbacks so painful that the soldier feels a need to end his/her life just to finally be at peace and halt the pain. I have never felt a need to take out my aggressions on myself or a loved one.

When asked to explain why I had less difficulty than some others in readjusting to civilian life upon my return from Vietnam, I give credit to several factors. Firstly, I had excellent nursing training with a serious hands-on education. I also spent nine months within the military nursing culture at Fort Dix, unlike some nurses who found themselves thrust into the war zone fresh out of training. In addition, though I saw horrific wounds, my role was to save and heal, not to kill and destroy. Finally, as I have mentioned, I returned to a small town in the Midwest, not a university campus ripe with protests. Traditionally, small town USA has generally praised its returning veterans. No parade after Vietnam, but still a community pride in having sent a local citizen off to war.

TEMPORARY FAMILY AND LOVERS

It has been said that friends are the family that you are allowed to choose. While I did not have an option to select with whom I would spend my year in Vietnam, I learned very early on in my tour that there were certain individuals that I would grow to consider family. One of the first things that became very clear to me was that I would need to rely on the friendship of my fellow medical personnel to survive what lay ahead. These were fellow vets who understood what all of us were living with. Few civilians back in the real world had a clue about life in the war. They could write that they loved you, prayed for you, and worried about your safety. But it was the person standing next to you around the litter of a bloodied GI who was asking if he was going to die, that knew the depth of your pain.

Friendships were formed quickly. "All's fair in love and war" is an often used expression. It takes on a much deeper meaning when you find yourself actually in a war setting. Your fellow staff members are like a unique fraternity or sorority, without the secret handshake. Each member covers for the other members of the group. Sharing was ubiquitous from care packages to personal concerns to on-duty responsibilities. At the same time, there were few secrets within the hospital. Just as everyone knows every other person's business in a tiny community, so the same was true at the 91st. Good or bad, one's life for that year was an open book.

While there was an unspoken military hierarchy as there is on any military compound, the rules were much less stringent on the battlefield. The only saluting that I could recall occurred when someone with the rank of general would happen by. I never experienced the doctors and nurses, who were all officers, being saluted by corpsmen. It just was not practical. There was always the standing rule that an officer was not to become romantically involved with an enlisted person though I personally knew of such relationships. (You simply could not keep a secret for long.)

It was true that after work the compound was fairly segregated as the docs and nurses headed to the Officers' club and the corpsmen to the NCO club. That is simply the way of the military. I do remember a few occasions when those lines blurred. I vaguely recall that someone acquired a record player and vinyl records of square dance music. Several of us were interested in joining in the merriment and gathered in a large empty shed for a few evenings to swing our partners! The dancers were a wide variety of individuals with no concern about status or rank.

Concerns about romantic liaisons have been a controversial topic for as long as members of the opposite sex have shared close quarters in the military. Add to the mix the stress of saving lives, repairing shattered bodies, and daily worrying about whether you would survive the next mortar attack and you have the perfect recipe for sexual attraction. Whether in novels, the movies, or on television, one often sees a plot built around the "I may not come back from this mission" thinking. In many of the scenarios, the drama builds around a passionate one-night stand with the handsome soldier pulling his uniform back on in the morning, casually draping his jacket over one shoulder, planting a last kiss and then disappearing into the morning mist. Yes, that probably did transpire from time to time, but most partnerships were far less glamorous. I did meet a few pilots during the year but avoided falling for the "one last mission" line.

There certainly was coupling within the hospital personnel, plenty of it. Some of those were strictly platonic while others were of a much more romantic nature. Some lasted a few weeks; others went on for months. There were also a few couples that continued their relationships and even married after returning to the States. I wonder how many of those marriages survived the test of time.

While in country, the one factor that tied each of us closely together was doing our job and making it home alive. Nothing more was needed. Once back home, the simple chores of daily living easily dimmed that passion of surviving together.

Over the years much has been discussed about women, especially in Vietnam, as well as subsequent conflicts, who were raped or otherwise taken advantage of. I have heard some serious allegations made by nurses, Red Cross workers, USO entertainers, and others who have alleged being the victims of sexual abuse by soldiers, most specifically by officers who outranked the individual being assaulted. One of the characters in the play "A Piece of my Heart," based on the experiences of six women who actually served in Vietnam, talks about being raped. Many cases have been documented and it certainly was something that did take place during the war. On a personal level, I was not aware of anyone during my time at the 91st who was the victim of such an attack. Given the environment and the ratio of males to females at the time, it should not come as a surprise that such events did occur.

For me, becoming romantically involved with another person was as much about the mental support as the physical love. There were two men who held a special place in my heart during my year overseas. The first was a hospital administrator who was from Mississippi. We met shortly after I arrived and seemed to instantly feel comfortable with each other. He shared a hootch with two other officers who were also involved in hospital administration. Much of our time together began with a group gathering early in the evening after working the day shift and ended with the two of us alone. Lots of talking, a bit of Mateus wine or scotch, and taped music from someone's recorder would easily result in us wrapped in each other's arms. We were a comfort to each other, especially on those days that were long and challenging.

Looking back, I believe that simply knowing that someone else was concerned about my well-being was the most important aspect of a one-on-one relationship. The realization that one special person would be there holding your hand, promising that you would be all right, was comforting.

As I said, we all were very much aware that most of us would only be in country for a year. Some of us remained in one place for the entire tour while others, depending on their MOS or job in the military, were reassigned to various units and locations in South Vietnam. That is precisely what happened to my close friend. After three months, he was transferred. No specific reason was given, but it did not matter. When you were told to move, that is what you did!

A few months later, I met a physician who had just arrived at the 91st. His specialty was anesthesiology but, at the hospital and particularly in the emergency room, all hands were needed, regardless of expertise. We found ourselves working side by side many days and nights. Gradually, we started spending time together after hours as well. It was a very easy relationship. I was immediately struck by his gentleness. I grew up in a world of men who were the head of the household and ruled the roost. Not abusive at all, just not what I would call gentle. The Army Engineer I dated at Ft. Dix, in retrospect, was abusive.

The anesthesiologist and I would remain close for the rest of my time in Vietnam. I left in October; his DEROS (date of expected return from overseas service) was not until April. He continued to write until he also had returned to "the world." We knew that there was no future relationship for us at that point, but I really feel that our time together served to keep both of us sane in an insane setting. I still have photos and letters that he wrote. Some things are just hard to part with because they shaped who we are and affected decisions made later in life. I had not read the letters in perhaps thirty years until I began researching materials for this book. I was so grateful that his letters helped me relive my past.

I DID WHAT?

In going through my journal from Vietnam, I came across several entries that caused me to query, "What was that all about?" For instance, on January 10, I had written, "sewed curtains." I have no idea what that refers to. Since I had no windows, I'm not sure where the curtains were hung unless they clothed the entire screen wall. I do remember using fabric, as I mentioned earlier, to cover my trunk. I have no clue where I acquired yard goods in the middle of a warzone, much less a means of sewing it into something useful. I have indeed been sewing since I was eight years old, but my memory of that particular incident has faded.

I did get rather creative with what little materials I had to work with. After a couple months, I sought to redecorate my tiny room. Think Martha Stewart in a combat zone. I purchased two of the ubiquitous conical Vietnamese hats. After cutting a four-inch round hole off the point of one and an eight-inch hole off the point of the other, I sewed the rims together. I then finished off the edges with some ribbon and dropped a bare light bulb down the center from the ceiling. Voila, a beautiful hanging lamp with a soft glow that showed off the patterns woven into the hat. It bathed my room in a lovely soft light. Mood lighting!

On another page, during the month of February, I penned, "Waxed floor of room periodically." While I have always favored a tidy environment, what was I thinking—waxing the floor of my room! Where did I get the wax?! Who was I trying to impress?! A later entry states, with emphasis, "Rat in room!" I do actually remember that incident because I awoke in the middle of the night to see this dark furry varmint scurrying across my quilt. He probably couldn't get any traction on my newly waxed floor and had to ascend to the bed to make progress.

There were several entries concerning specific individuals who shall remain unnamed in this book. Some of those bits would come under the "what" category. One group of four guys on the hospital administration staff formed a team to pull pranks on others and thus help us to forget the war for a while. They would undertake what became known as RPP missions. While not at all politically correct today, that stood for "rape, pillage and plunder." There was really no raping or pillaging at all. Plundering, perhaps. Generally they took it upon themselves to orchestrate a type of shivery outside your room at 2:00 in the morning to celebrate your birthday or a promotion. When a new arrival came to the hospital, they greeted him or her with a special ceremony, which involved placing a plunger with an attached white flag on your head while someone read the rules of the compound. All was carried out in fun and followed by several rounds of toasts with whatever libation was at hand. To the outside world, this probably would seem like very immature behavior for grown men. Remember, we had to make our own entertainment. Creativity was highly prized!

INCONVENIENCES? IT WAS A WARZONE, AFTER ALL!

While being assigned to a field hospital was not exactly a luxury existence we did have access to many of life's basic needs that eluded the guys out in the bush. Real food, showers, sheets and pillows, a roof over our heads, and a change of clothes were just a few of our benefits. There were episodes, however, when even these simple pleasures vanished into thin air.

There were times when the water system went down, usually seconds after you had just worked up a good lather of shampoo on your dirty locks. What to do? Grab one of the 5-gallon metal cans of stored water and pour it over your sudsy head. As the water was unheated, you could expect to catch your breath and yelp loudly enough to bring someone running to inquire if it was a mouse or cold water that brought forth the scream. No matter the warmth of the day, it took several minutes to subdue the shivering.

The cuisine of the mess hall bested the c-rations that the guys in the field lived on. Yet there was much room for improvement. When I worked nights, you could take a brief break around midnight and head to the mess hall for powdered eggs and coffee with toast. Some of the highlights (or sidelights) of lunch and dinner were Jello, mashed potatoes, and bacon. Gelatin, in temperatures above 100 degrees fahrenheit, quickly undergoes a change of appearance and consistency from a gel to a liquid. You needed a straw rather than a spoon to eat it. Mashed potatoes, while tasty, are not colorful. To accommodate the person who likes a "pretty" meal, they often garnished the large metal tray of white potatoes with glossy red maraschino cherries! An interesting treat for the taste buds! Of course, the problem with the bacon was that it was limp as a rag, never crispy.

As far as shopping was concerned, it stands to reason that one would not expect to find a shopping mall in the midst of battle. There was a post exchange (PX) on each of the larger compounds and hospital grounds. Unfortunately, the inventory selections left much to be desired. On any given day, one could purchase men's pants hangers or outdated Playboy magazines, while necessary items such as soap or toothpaste were often hard to find. I even chose my diamond engagement ring at the PX in Chu Lai.

One might question including this lighthearted chapter in a memoir about a tragic war and it's place in our country's history. Yet, this was my day-to-day existence for a full year of my life. In an attempt to leave a legacy for my children and grandchildren, I felt that it was important to cover all aspects of my time in Vietnam. Everyone's experience was a bit different; this was mine.

MARRY ME?

When I was stationed at Ft. Dix, I began dating a young man in the Corps of Engineers. He had already served in Vietnam and was due to return to civilian life in a few months when I received orders for the warzone. He told me that he might "re-up" just so he could go back to Nam and be with me. I considered that craziness and did not really expect him to follow through. I also was ambivalent about my feelings concerning our relationship. While the men that I knew within my family and among my parents' friends were NOT abusive, they were, in my opinion, not always warm and fuzzy. While they may have had soft centers, they were a bit rough around the edges. When I left home, I just assumed that was the way most men were.

After dating JC, as I shall call him, for a while, I discovered that he had a mean streak, especially after a few scotch and waters. Most of his "bad boy" behavior was verbal—loud and argumentative which made me very uncomfortable when it occurred in public. Of course, even after a turbulent evening's date, the next day was filled with apologies and kind words. I was thrilled to have someone to share in my new life and career. We went to lavish parties, celebrated promotions and special events with champagne at the Officers' Club, and made a handsome couple. For four weeks in early spring, he was assigned TDY to Camp Drum, N.Y., not far from the Canadian border. I would request a weekend pass, climb in my Rambler American, and make the three hundred and fifty mile drive to spend two and a half days in the barren isolated outpost before returning to Ft Dix. Once I spun out on the ice glazed highway as I nodded off trying to get back in time to avoid being AWOL. On another occasion, I ran out of gas at 3:00 in the morning and had to summon the local police chief who woke up a filling station owner. He filled my tank so I could be on my way. (In 1969 there were no all-night truck stops.)

Indeed, I was fond of JC, maybe even thought that I was in love. Then, a few weeks before I left to go on leave prior to my departure for Vietnam, we had had dinner with another couple and were all back in my apartment for a nightcap. JC had had several scotches and something that was said did not sit well with him. I don't remember what caused his rage, but he picked up a chair and threw it at me, catching me off guard. Fortunately, our friends overtook him and hustled him back to his BOQ, leaving me to wonder what to do next. It was only one time and I was certain, as are so many women in troubled relationships, that it would not happen again. Still, I was hesitant. I was accustomed to men being tough and forceful; I wasn't ready to call him abusive. I just wasn't sure.

Thus, when I learned in January that he really was coming back to Vietnam after signing up for another year, I had mixed feelings. I was not the same person that had said goodbye to him eight months prior. I had found "love" in someone else that had nothing to do with forcefulness or "being in charge." Yet, here was someone that was so enamored with me that he was willing to return to a combat setting to be with me! This was more than just jumping on a plane to fly across the country to propose. This was flying 10,000 miles to a dangerous combat zone to risk one's life for love! Could this really be happening?

Yet, as I got word of his intentions, life at the hospital

went on, paying no attention to my personal conundrum. Some of my journal entries gave testimony to our daily routine: "Crazy busy! Frag wounds. GI conscious, but back stayed on litter when we tried to roll him over. Alive into OR." The next evening we celebrated my birthday with a party at one of the doctor's hootches (the "Villa") with snacks, spirits, music and merriment. Life went on…

When JC did show up on March 13, I recorded that I sensed that something was different; I did not feel the same love for him as I had back in the States. I struggled with making a decision. We did pick out a diamond ring, even ordered a bright blue Olds Cutlass to be delivered to a dealership near my hometown when I returned. We got a weekend pass and drove to Hue "for fun." We officially announced our engagement in my local newspaper. Together, in August, we spent our R&R in Hong Kong—a romantic, exciting city. Two weeks later, I broke off our engagement. The five months that we had spent together made me realize that I had indeed changed. No longer was I enamored by pure physical attraction. I wanted to spend time with a kind, even-tempered man, not someone who was unpredictable and short-tempered. Looking back on my decision, I realize just how right it was. I have never regretted ending that relationship.

THE WAR ESCALATES

Beginning around Easter Sunday 1970, which fell on the

29th of March, enemy activity around our area seemed to increase significantly. My journal noted that we had an early morning alert and then remained on alert for two days. During those times, we were instructed to be more aware of our surroundings, to stay on the hospital compound, and to be ready for heavier casualties. The tension was palpable as we kept up our daily routines, but eyed every Vietnamese arrival with greater scrutiny. Breaks were cancelled; casualties mounted. My calendar showed that I was halfway through my tour. I could only guess what the second half of my time there was going to be like.

Though statistics indicate that the United States started pulling troops out of Vietnam in April of 1969, our flood of causalities did not slow down, but actually increased during my deployment. On April 30, 1970, the hospital compound was hit at 1150 that morning. Fortunately, there were no major injuries, but it brought the war even closer, making us realize that nowhere was truly safe. Four days later, my entry reads, "We got hit! 0600 to 0700. Beaucoup casualties all day." It was a bloody day with lots of Vietnamese civilians wounded as well as GI casualties and fatalities. Everyone was called to duty; breaks were just long enough for a cigarette or a latrine visit.

The enemy was getting an early start at celebrating Uncle Ho's birthday on May 6. Uncle Ho was Ho Chi Minh, the leader of the North Vietnamese people. He was revered in the north and his troops expressed their allegiance by terrorizing South Vietnamese residents and the foreign troops supporting them with daybreak rocket attacks. For two days in a row, the sirens went off at 0600. As we grabbed our steel pots and flak jackets, we could hear the mortars screaming overhead. Their intensity increased the second day, but fortunately, most of the rounds landed in the South China Sea. The high-pitched whistle followed by a watery splash is a sound that I have never forgotten! I recorded the attack with this passage, "Got hit again at 0600. Closer this time. Very tired. Expecting hit tonight. Scared!"

May 6 dawned quietly with no sirens or sounds of whistling missiles. Perhaps everyone was taking off for Uncle Ho's birthday, enjoying a bit of cake and ice cream! We tried to picture Ho wearing a brightly colored pointy party hat, his scraggly graying beard caught up in the elastic chinstrap! A humorous image indeed.

Whether Uncle Ho celebrated in a grand style or not, we soon found out that his supporters were not yet finished with their display of force. The next two days would prove to be among my most exhausting. Clearly the North was not going to give us a break for more than one day. On May 7 at 0115, we were overwhelmed with a mass casualty situation. For the next twenty-four hours, the R & E was a study of organized chaos as we treated 99 patients, many of them civilians. Their village had been attacked. Tiny babies, elderly grandparents, and school children, all were needing medical attention.

We placed the more seriously injured on litters on the floor and outdoor sidewalks. All physicians and emergency room staff were called in. Most of the wounds were the result of flying shrapnel from splintered buildings and destroyed equipment. Everyone who was assigned to the R&E, regardless of what their scheduled shift was for that day, hurried to the hospital. I worked for my usual twelve hours plus several more.

Caring for so many victims is always a challenge, but doing so without command of their language made it even more difficult. Most of us knew a few basic words like "nuoc" for water and "dau" for pain, but that did not help greatly. The hospital did have two interpreters that provided much needed assistance. Also on duty from time to time were a Vietnamese nurse and an aide. Just having a kind soul who spoke the same language and could reassure the injured that their pleas were being heard was most beneficial. Unfortunately, with so many wounded at one time, they were overwhelmed like the rest of us.

Our first monumental challenge was triage. Most days, one physician would be in charge of the order in which patients were readied for surgery, depending on the injury. He might seek advice from a second doctor should one be present. On that day, each decision was a collective one. The dialog was fast and furious. "I have a bad head wound over here that needs to be at the front of the line." "Here is a possible amputation of the right leg. Tourniquet in place, but we are going to need a couple units (of blood)." "This fellow appears to be in serious pain though I can't find an obvious wound. Must be something internally." "I need a translator over here please!" "Ask her where it hurts." Watching the agony on a parent's face as her child whimpered with pain was heartbreaking.

As the light of day faded, we were still admitting patients, patching up the less severely wounded, comforting those in pain, and attempting to keep records on our blood smeared notebooks. Several of us were asked to give blood, which was in short supply. By dawn, the floor was finally hosed clean of the last remnants of human suffering. Shelves were restocked with IV bottles, bandages, chest tubes, and splints. The Vietnamese ward was bursting at the seams with beds filling every free inch of floor space. The cries and moans had softened with the aid of pain meds and the soothing voices of the staff and family who had come along with the victims.

I stumbled back to my room, anxious to slip out of my blood-soaked fatigues and shower away 12 hours of sweat and dust. Collapsing onto my creaky bed, sleep overcame my fatigue as I closed my eyes and ears to the war. Back home they were continuing the draw down of troops; here in the war, the violence raged on.

A TWO DAY ESCAPE

In June, when I was still undecided about my feelings for

JC, who had suddenly returned to my world, I did meet up with him for a couple days away from the hospital. The "outing" involved a flight to DaNang for me to join him and a buddy on a day trip to Hue. The city was the provincial capital during the French occupation and, at its center, was the Citadel, the palace of some of the Vietnamese kings who ruled prior to that. While we gave little thought to the possibility of mines or snipers, we did take flak jackets and steel pots along as a precaution. An M-16 was nestled in the back seat of the Jeep next to me. The weather was rainy and gray, but the trek did afford us a terrific means of experiencing everyday life in the country. It also gave us a change of scenery and a sense of "getting away" even if it was not very far or the least bit luxurious.

Our journey turned into a photographic expedition for me as I captured on film Vietnamese citizens going about their daily activities almost as if there was not a vicious war surrounding them. I shot images of local markets where women displayed freshly-picked vegetables and fruits, butchers hung slabs of raw bacon and carcasses of cattle, and children hawked everything from pencils to candies. Every few kilometers, tiny open-air eateries with equally diminutive plastic chairs offered pho and other assorted traditional Vietnamese fare. We drove past rice paddies where water buffalo plodded along cultivating the muddy soil as they had for centuries, during conflicts and peacetime.

Occasionally we spied a roadside "refreshment stand" where one could purchase a can or bottle of something liquid—beer, pop, and juice. We were always cautioned to not patronize such stands as the cans were often boo-by-trapped and the bottles refilled after prior use. This was before the days of the ubiquitous bottled water but the canteens that we had filled ourselves worked quite well and were much safer.

Hue had some lovely architecture to photograph. The Catholic cathedral, which survived all of the war years and which I revisited in 1996, stood tall with a unique steeple. The Art Museum, which also survived, was a vision with its large pillars though desperately in need of a fresh coat of white paint. It was, however, the fishing nets thrown by local fishermen that I found most beautiful along the Hai Van Pass, our route from DaNang to Hue. As we came down from the forested mountains, the water spread out before us in soothing shades of pastels, blues and pinks, a most tranquil scene. I am certain that the fishing was hard labor, but the peaceful feeling made it seem less so.

The photographs that I took that weekend are an important part of my presentation when I speak to students and civic organizations about my year in the war. They provide a perfect balance to tales of combat, the wounded and killed. They serve to remind us that life went on in so many villages and cities despite the ever-present war. That special weekend in 1970, though, gave three soldiers a much-needed break from the perils of war. Having revisited the Hai Van Pass as recently as October 2014, it was reassuring to see that the landscape in that part of the country has continued to have a tranquil sense about it.

R&R IN HONG KONG

While the weekend in Hue was a brief respite from the war, a month later, in July 1970, I spent 10 days in Hong Kong, enjoying a serious vacation from the war. What an exciting city it was! Each time someone returned from R&R (rest and recreation), we would gather around, anxious to hear his/her stories about the flashy nightlife, wonderful food, custom-made clothing, and inexpensive stereo equipment purchased and shipped home. JC, by then my fiancé, would be joining me, sharing the same room. Looking back 44 years, this was not the smartest decision that I have made in my lifetime, but it did help me come to a definitive answer about where our relationship was headed.

Though I have returned to Hong Kong since that first visit, there is nothing more memorable than the initial burst of neon colors and the intoxicating haze of aromas that greets you when you disembark your plane in this crowded metropolis, especially when you have just come from an olive green, red dust, defoliated country. Its vertical landscape of skyscrapers and brightly lighted signs like colored markers in a giant box was a treat for the eyes. Then there were the cries of shop owners hawking their wares on the sidewalk promising, "For you, first time in Hong Kong, the very best deal."

Such deals there were—watches for ten dollars, hand carved wooden fruit for six dollars, intricate "Army/Navy tablecloths" (named for the alternating blocks of lace and embroidery). There was jewelry of every type, semi-precious stones, gold, silver and, sad to say, ivory. I still wear some of the rings and necklaces that I purchased over forty years ago. Electronics were a hot commodity because one could find the latest in speakers, turntables, and tuners and then have them all shipped home. Most everyone bought at least one piece.

The most sought after experience, however, was having clothes tailor-made in less than two days. The guys ordered suits and dress shirts, even shoes and boots. I chose suede for a coat, several pieces of the softest wool for some dresses and skirts, silk and satin for blouses, and even beautiful leather for boots that I wore for at least a decade. The craftsmanship was very high quality; I've not seen anything for the price to compare since! My final purchase was very special. I bought several meters of raw silk that I would eventually sew, creating my gorgeous wedding gown.

The eight days flew by quickly as we dined well, rode the ferry, took a city tour, and ventured outside of Hong Kong to see the mountain range separating communist

China (known at that time as Red China) from Hong Kong. Everyone who took his/her R&R in this location, made that trip. We photographed the junks in Aberdeen Harbor, had lunch on the floating Jumbo restaurant, and took the tram up Victoria Peak for the best view of the city.

It was an adventure not to be forgotten, but I realized that the person who accompanied me was not someone that I wanted to spend the rest of my life with. Five days after we returned to Vietnam, I broke off our engagement.

SWEET SORROW

William Shakespeare, in Romeo and Juliet, penned a much used phrase, "Parting is such sweet sorrow." I could not think of a better way to describe my feelings upon leaving Vietnam. When sharing my thoughts with young students, I liken my tour in Vietnam to a year-long summer camp. You make very close friends during your time together and it is heartbreaking to bid everyone farewell. Of course, war is not summer camp, but the personal ties formed are suddenly split apart when your tour is up. One day you are working alongside those who have been your closest companions and the next day you are on your way to the airport. You talk of reunions and planned visits in the future, knowing that the chances are quite good that they will not take place.

For some returning vets, leaving their units and fellow soldiers behind filled them with a different emotion—guilt. They were going home, in one piece, while others were struggling to survive in a hospital or, worse yet, were flown back in a flag-draped coffin. "Why him and not me?" was the question that vets often expressed upon arriving back home. For most of us, we were just grateful that we had survived our year without major injuries and would live to see our family and friends back home. Alas for many, their homecoming in the States was far from what they had hoped it would be.

I remember well my dear friend and close companion driving me to the airport in Chu Lai for a flight to Cam Rahn Bay. It was a hot, sticky day, so typical of the past year. My tears fell in rivulets, mixing with the billowing clouds of red dust kicked up by the jeep. As we prepared to leave the 91st, he took just one photo of me with the helipad of the hospital in the background. I had forgotten about the photo until it surfaced recently. Staring back at me was a somber faced young woman who had seen so much and matured beyond her 23 years. I was on my way to board a "freedom bird" which would carry me back to "the world" and my family. For some returning vets, coming home to the States was more painful then getting orders for deployment to Vietnam in the first place. A small percentage of these vets "re-upped," meaning they signed on for another tour of duty so they could go back to Vietnam where they actually felt more comfortable. They found upon their return to the United States that they had little in common with those they had bid farewell to the year before. Their souls were still in Vietnam, in the war. Unless personally experienced, one can never know just how heart-wrenching that final goodbye really was.

SEATAC

My return from Vietnam aboard a Flying Tiger airplane (used for cargo but refitted to fly troops) was uneventful except that I was the only female vet aboard. I changed out of my fatigues and into my corded greens. I tossed my combat boots in a trash barrel before boarding the plane. Sort of a rite of passage, though I wished later that I had brought them back. I also left my cigarettes behind though I did take a puff, on rare occasions, for the next couple years. That bad habit was dropped several decades ago.

We arrived at SeaTac airport in Washington State and I processed out of the Army at Ft. Lewis. My official ETS (estimated time of separation) was 10 October 1970. There was lots of paperwork to fill out before I could actually leave. I do remember spending a night in the airport. During that time period, there was a special area available for military personnel to use if needed. It housed cots and food to accommodate those who were in transit. It was much appreciated after the lengthy flight and emotional goodbyes of the previous days. Home, was however, where I really wanted to be.

Forty-eight hours later, I was on a TWA plane to St. Louis where my mom met me. I do not recall much about those first days back though I think that I slept a lot. I had ordered several items through PACEX (Pacific Exchange), the mail order service for items that you did not want to carry home——china tableware and brass candlesticks. Also waiting for me was my guitar, the electronic equipment shipped from Hong Kong, and the beautiful clothes that I had tailored, ready for me to enjoy in the cool fall weather. It was a bit like an early Christmas and I was excited to show my family what I had purchased.

How strange it felt to be back in an environment that I had left nearly a year ago. The weather was getting cold; in Vietnam, the coolest days were only in the lower 60s. While that is cold in Vietnam, it was warm compared to the 30s and 40s of the Midwest. Loud noises—cars backfiring, balloons popping, and doors slamming—all sent me diving to the floor for cover. Simply climbing behind the wheel of a car and starting the engine was a practice that I had not done in a year. Easing my way into interstate traffic caused my hands to clench the steering wheel so tightly that my knuckles blanched. There were the little habits acquired while I was living in a tropical climate, such as banging the salt shaker on the table to loosen the clumps or devouring food at a record pace to enjoy Jello when it was still in its wiggly state, that my family found curious.

But the biggest adjustment was realizing that no one back home wanted to talk about Vietnam and my year away. Personally, I did not suffer the taunts and insults that many of the returning vets did. I came home to a small town where it was an honor to serve in the military, even in this very unpopular war. My father was disappointed that I would not join the American Legion Post back home. I think he really wanted his daughter to be one of the few women to become a member of the organization. Since I did not plan on staying in Mascoutah for years, it did not seem practical to join an organization made up of mostly men my father's age. I was not even staying in town for a few weeks as I had made plans with another nurse at the 91st to continue exploring possibilities for employment now that we were both out of the service. I don't know if my folks were disappointed that I didn't settle in for a few months upon my return. There was very little discussion, or at least none that I recall, concerning my future plans. They did know that I was planning to go to Denver to seek employment as I had informed them of that before I left Vietnam. I suspect they probably just accepted that I was a grown woman and would be making my own decisions now. As far as my father was concerned, as long as I was employed, he was satisfied!

Before I left Vietnam, I had befriended another nurse who had her eyes on Fitzsimmons Army Hospital in Denver, as I did. Our hope was to be employed as civil-service nurses at the hospital as we would both be out of the military at that point. We were comfortable with military nursing and, secretly, I had hoped to be working with soldiers who had returned from the field but needed additional care just as I had done at Ft Dix. Since Becky had returned to the States a few months before I did, it was agreed that when I got back I would fly to Minneapolis near her home and we would embark on a driving trip, throughout the Northwest, ultimately ending up in Denver. At that point, we were hoping to land jobs at the beginning of the New Year. Thus, in the middle of November, I flew to Minneapolis, spent a couple nights with my friend and her family and then we were off on a great adventure. The one significant event that took place while we were in Minneapolis was the opening of the movie *M.A.S.H.* at a local drive-in theater. We went and had an uproarious time—laughing one minute, sobbing the next, happy to be back, but missing friends and co-workers back in Nam. We were both grateful that the showing was at a drive-in and not the walk-in regular theater. I suspect we would have been kicked out for our emotional outbursts.

The six weeks that we spent on the road turned out to be very therapeutic for me and the perfect way to reengage with the real world. For some returning females, the very act of integrating themselves into the social scene in the States was a shock. Being very much the minority sex in Vietnam, we were accustomed to being the "belles of the ball." At parties on the hospital compound, we never sat out a dance. The attention was something that we came to expect. Back in the States, we were just one of many females vying for a chance to grace the dance floor. The spotlight was no longer on "the nurses" and it was upsetting to many.

Heading out in her family's manual shift Chevy, our first stop was in the Black Hills of South Dakota. We marveled in the artistry of Mount Rushmore with its cap of glistening November snow. As we prepared to leave, we discovered that our parking brake had frozen during our brief visit. With a casual mention about our past year to other tourists, we had no trouble finding men willing to help thaw it out. Heading west, we drove through Yellowstone without seeing another car for 70 miles. In Cody, Wyoming we faced blizzard conditions and got snowed in in Boise, Idaho. We laughed, drank a bit, and recorded our thoughts on little mini tape reels that, unfortunately, have also become lost with the passage of time. Fortunately, I kept a journal so I knew where we went, whom we were with, and what we did.

The plan for this journey included, when possible, staying with nurses we had met in Vietnam who, like ourselves, had just returned from the war. Our first visit was to a nurse who had been assigned to our hospital and lived in Seattle. We spent a couple nights, shared war stories, and caught up on the latest news from the 91st. Heading south, we moved on to Portland, San Francisco, and Los Angeles where each time we stayed with former Vietnam nurses. I did not record everything in my journal but I do remember meeting a guy in a bar in Los Angeles and accepting his invitation to go back to his apartment. He ran out of gas driving me back in the wee hours of the morning to where I was staying. I did make it back safely, for which I am most grateful.

We spent some time in Las Vegas after leaving California and enjoyed a couple shows while sipping Cold Duck. It didn't get much better than that! After two days we motored on to our next destination, over a very snowy Loveland Pass through the Rockies where the car stalled going uphill. It was yet another memorable event of our trip that finally got us to Denver and Fitzsimmons Army hospital. We applied for employment as civil-service nurses and were both accepted. A month later, January 1971, the next phase of our lives would begin as we returned to nursing. Little did I realize the life-changing events that that year would have in store for me!

MYSTERY ILLNESS

The entire six weeks that we had been on the road, I was suffering from intense headaches as well as numbness and tingling in my legs. As I kept ingesting Darvon Compound to ease the pain, I knew that I had to seek medical advice when I got back to Mascoutah. I started my search with the VA hospital near my home but, after spending an entire day sitting in a room and getting no attention, I gave up the ship and found myself in a civilian hospital for my first Christmas home from Vietnam. It was not a place that I wanted to be, especially having been away from my family for a year. The one bright spot was my roommate, an older woman who was very kind and understanding of my situation. We actually exchanged Christmas cards for many years after that. For five days, I underwent numerous tests and procedures including a myelogram, spinal tap, and blood studies, all with negative results. My symptoms finally dissipated without a confirmed diagnosis, but it stole my precious Christmas at home.

While no cause was found for my headaches in 1970, 45 years later I would learn that I had Parkinson's disease. After exhaustive research, the Veterans Administration admitted that exposure to Agent Orange could result in Parkinson's disease. I am grateful that they accepted the claim that I filed and pleased that they have finally admitted accountability for those of us now living with Parkinson's and many other life-altering conditions.

DENVER

The first week of January 1971, I packed up my worldly possessions and headed to Denver. Becky and I were assigned to different areas of Fitzsimmons. While she got placed on an orthopedic ward working with GIs who had returned from Vietnam but needed further hospitalization, I was assigned to a female medical floor with patients whose health concerns were vastly removed from the type of injuries that I had treated in Vietnam. After a year of fast-paced, intense nursing, I missed the guys and the adrenaline rush of combat medicine. Though I continued to practice on that ward, I was not heartbroken when eventually I had to leave it behind.

Life in Colorado was punctuated in the early 70s with skiing, biking, and lots of small clubs featuring folk music performers. For a $2.50 cover charge or two drinks, one could sit and sip all evening while hearing some great music. John Denver, Linda Ronstadt, and Jimmy Webb were just a few. I was excited to be a part of it, despite my unhappy nursing assignment. Becky and I got an apartment in a "Singles only" complex, each hoping to meet a tall dark handsome skier and spend the rest of our lives on the slopes.

About six months after arriving in Denver, I did meet

someone who would change my life. He wasn't a skier, however. As a matter of fact, he had never been on skis, much less pointed them downhill and schussed away. He was a young lawyer from the Kansas City area who was fulfilling his Army Reserve requirement in a medical unit, hoping to avoid having to serve a tour in Vietnam. He was assigned to work on the floor at Fitzsimmons where I was the charge nurse. We met over a patient; he kept reminding me that his name was Jim, not Eisenbrandt. Even though I was working nights at the time, we went out each evening for a week. I flew to Kansas City to spend a weekend, he proposed a month later back in Denver, and we were married five months later on November 20. From the mountain peaks of the Rockies, through the flat prairie grassland of western Kansas, to suburbia in Overland Park, I was, once again, seeing another part of the world. That was my goal after all!

HAPPILY EVER AFTER

As I pen this, Jim and I just celebrated our forty-third wedding anniversary, have two grown children and two precious grandchildren. We've not moved far from our first apartment, shared space with four dogs over the years, worked and volunteered in local communities, and enjoyed life. Our real passion though is for travel. I've never lost my desire to visit destinations far and wide; Jim has embraced my wanderings. Over the years we have tossed coins in the Trevi Fountain in Rome, hiked Machu Picchu, ridden an elephant in India, and swam with sea lions in the Galapagos. Our soirees have taken us from the Amazon to Africa and soon will land us in Australia. While all of these trips were shared adventures, in December 1994, I left Jim behind and joined a small group of travel agents to return to Vietnam for the first time since the war.

RETURN TRIP NUMBER ONE—
CURIOSITY

I had been curious for many years about what had become of the country that had known so much war but was slowly reuniting its opposing halves even though it remained under communist rule. Working as a travel agent in the mid-90s, I was offered an opportunity, for a reasonable price, to find out. The United States lifted its embargo in 1994 and Vietnam was seeking tourists to enhance the country's coffers. As our Vietnam Airlines plane landed in Saigon (renamed Ho Chi Minh City but still referred to by many by its older name), the large concrete bunkers used during the war to store helicopters were visible lining the sides of the runways. A gentle rain producing droplets on the plane window set the mood for this return visit, mimicking the quiet tears trailing down my cheeks. From the Mekong Delta, oppressively steamy in the heat of the day to the cooling breezes that

I remembered from my year at the 91st on the cliff over-looking the South China Sea, and further upward over the Hai Van pass on our journey to Hue, I was going to relive many memories—positive as well as unpleasant. Our group's final stop was north of the former DMZ. We would visit Hanoi and Halong Bay, places now open to tourists but with a cooler climate and less colorful population than southern Vietnam.

The feelings among Vietnam veterans about return-ing to the country where they experienced so much pain, lost many friends, and witnessed unimaginable atrocities, vary widely. Some want to have nothing to do with that part of their past. Others are uncertain even when offered the opportunity to return. Still, some vets, like myself, felt a need to return, whether just out of curiosity or to bring closure to a difficult period in our lives and the na-tion's history. I felt that the trip(s) back, in my case four, were cathartic. In addition to discovering that the Viet-namese people have not held a grudge against Americans, including vets, I also received that "Welcome Home" upon returning to the U.S. that I never got the first time. On my final visit in September 2014, we were greeted by a band upon arrival at KCI, even though it was midnight when our delayed flight finally arrived! There were no bands, no balloons, and no TV cameras when I returned in 1970.

The other twelve travel agents that I joined on that first trip back were very protective of my feelings and well-being. They all wanted to buy me a BaBaBa (333 in Vietnamese) beer at the outdoor bar at the top of the Rex Hotel in Saigon. The space had changed little in the 25 years since my last beer there the night before we flew to Hong Kong for R&R. I gladly accepted one beer, fearing that having more than one was a thing of the past! They also watched for my reaction to situations like crawling through the tunnels of Cu Chi and hearing a sudden loud noise, whether firecrackers or just a fallen book. I was surprised that so little had changed but was reminded that the U.S. had only lifted our embargo of Vietnam a few months prior to our visit. There were also a very limited number of foreigners traveling through the country. Most were young backpackers from Australia. Highway One, still the only paved road running the length of the country, was a giant traffic jam of cyclos, motorbikes toting entire families, lambrettas crammed with people, pigs and poultry, and busses in various stages of disrepair sporting extra passengers sitting on top of bundles on the roof. We visited markets, toured the Citadel in Hue, boated in the delta, and experienced a traditional water puppet show.

As we finished our trip heading across the old DMZ into what was "North Vietnam" during the war, the stark difference between north and south became clear. A colder climate and more austere landscape presented itself. The French influence was evident, but the American influence from music to colorful fabrics to lighthearted laughter was missing. We filed silently past Uncle Ho's preserved body, used public restrooms that were just small holes in a tiled floor with a nearby hose, and endured the Maison Centrale prison museum (aka "Hanoi Hilton"), with its propaganda about the treatment of American POWs. A couple of us quietly slipped into the back of the building to snap a photo of the few remaining prison cells as demolition teams were razing the building and its horrible memories. When I returned my last time in September 2014, I would find a very different scene.

RETURN TRIP NUMBER TWO— CLOSURE

After returning to the States from that trip, I knew that I had to make at least one more foray into Vietnam, to get as close as possible to where my hospital had been. I sought to reimagine, just once more, what my life had been like in 1969 and 1970 while standing on the sandy shore just a few kilometers away from where the 91st had stood. I had heard that the entire hospital, as well as the Americal Division compound with its amphitheater, planes, helicopters, and numerous buildings had been razed; yet I needed that closure. I also sensed that, with the normalization of relations with Vietnam on July 11, 1995, the country and its historical past would quickly begin to change. I needed one more look before that happened.

On January 18, 1996, in the middle of a plane-grounding snowstorm, a girlfriend and I were able to get on one of only two flights that left the Kansas City airport that afternoon to begin our journey. I had decided that I would make the return trip by myself if no one else could join me. My husband was in trial, but a long time friend accepted my offer, though she knew little about the country. As with all my trips to Asia, the lengthy flights were the toughest part, averaging twenty-four hours in the air plus time on the ground. We arrived in Saigon tired but excited. The tour company that had sponsored my trip the previous year had also set up this one with a guide who was a college student when the war ended in April 1975. Along with stops at some of the same venues that I had visited the year before, we added two new locations. My Lai, the site of the horrendous massacre of Vietnamese families in a small hamlet in 1968 by U.S. soldiers was our first destination. Chu Lai was the second.

The memorials to those killed at My Lai are in the form of tombstones set in the remaining foundations of each tiny home with the names of the deceased family members inscribed in the stone. There is a small museum with heart wrenching photos of the carnage following the attack. The gray, drizzly sky served as a fitting backdrop as we walked the ghostly grounds. That day remains engrained in my mind forever.

As we made our way north on Highway One, there

was discussion between our young driver and Cong, our seasoned guide. They were debating the risk of going to Chu Lai as it was now a Vietnamese military base. As we passed the old, original gate to the compound, our car suddenly turned off the highway and bounced along a pothole riddled dirt road. Cong told us to reply "tourist" should we be approached by guards. After several tense minutes, we stopped and Cong said, "Get out. Hurry!" I glanced at my friend and could tell she was not budging. I jumped out, ran toward the beach and began snapping photos, as quickly as I could. When our two guides finished relieving themselves in the trees, the three of us climbed back into the car and we made our way back to the highway. I realized just how far off the beaten path we really were when we stopped in a tiny village where they were building wooden fishing boats. The children that gathered to check us out were enamored with my friend. They had never seen anyone with blue eyes and blond hair!

As on my previous trip, we ventured north to Hanoi, spending a night on the way in Halong Bay with its captivating underwater mountains and caves. Yet undiscovered by most of the world, there were only two boats plying the waters. Nor did we see another American during our entire stay in the country. However, I had gotten as close as I possibly could to the now extinct hospital. I was grateful and pleased that I had made the trip.

RETURN TRIP NUMBER THREE—
SHARING

The opportunity to go back yet another time to Vietnam was the result of my husband's association with an international organization of attorneys. Each year, the group travels to a different part of the globe to learn about the legal system, practices, and customs of a foreign country. In September 2013, that trip was to Southeast Asia—Vietnam, Cambodia, northern Thailand, and Myanmar. For nearly a month we were pampered, wined, and dined at some of the most prestigious resorts in those countries. Our accommodations were of the five-star variety and, as is often true on these excursions, we were privileged to experience events not often open to tourists. In Vietnam, I did begin with my BaBaBa beer at the top of the Rex Hotel. Once more, I crawled through the Cu Chi tunnels, ate Elephant Ear fish in the delta, and strolled on China Beach. But now the tunnels were crowded with tourists and the beach walk was right outside our hotel door. So much building and commercialization had taken place since 1996 that I had difficulty recognizing landmarks.

Several of those in our group of approximately 100 travelers preferred the quiet and more moderate climate of the north to the noisy urban raucousness of the south. One thing that we all agreed upon was the beauty of Halong Bay where some of us spent the night on a 100-passenger vessel. I hardly recognized the setting however. Twenty years ago, there were just two boats on the water. Now the bay teemed with life and dozens of boats of all shapes and sizes. Several large caves had been discovered in the underwater mountains in recent years and, with the addition of vivid light displays, were attracting travelers from around the world.

Traces of the war were still easy to find in the war museums, both in Hanoi and Saigon. Memorials to both South and North Vietnamese soldiers who lost their lives in the war were scattered across the countryside. Occasionally one would encounter an aging shop owner or peddler whose stumps were evidence of having stepped on a land mine many years ago. With the passage of time, these sightings have decreased though there are still injuries being suffered as a result of undiscovered land mines. Several individuals and aid organizations have made it their life's ambition to locate and destroy these evil devices. When the president of the group we were traveling with asked me to address my fellow travelers and share my experiences, I was pleased to present a personal view as someone who had served during the war.

RETURN TRIP NUMBER FOUR— FELLOW VETS

Having made the third visit to Vietnam in 2013, I assumed that it was my last opportunity to explore that piece of my past. Much to my amazement and delight, however, in spring of 2014, I was once again given another chance. It was an offer that I could not ignore.

Since 2009, the College of the Ozarks in southern Missouri, has been undertaking a program that offers veterans the opportunity to return to the site of their service during a time of war. Previous trips had taken WWII and Korean vets to places in Europe, the South Pacific, Korea, and the Philippines. In September 2014, they would be making their first trip with vets returning to Vietnam. There would be 12 veterans, partnered with 12 students as well as a few faculty members, including the President and Vice-president. We would be traveling for two weeks, covering outposts and bases from the Mekong Delta to the central highlands to the coastal sites of DaNang and Chu Lai. Our final stop would be the Hanoi Hilton museum. As an added bonus, the college was covering all expenses! In agreeing to be part of this historical adventure, I learned that there had only been two women who had previously gone on one of these trips, both were WACS from WWII. I would be the first nurse and the only female veteran on this trip. I was excited and looking forward to our departure in September.

Emotional, comfortable, informational, memorable—the trip was all of these and much more. Just as any group with shared interests, we quickly slid into the "language of war." There was talk of APCs, LZs, C-rations and P38s. From our first greetings at the airport, the discussions were about where one was located in Nam, what hill did they overtake, how miserable the monsoon rains made life in the jungle. In our group, were two former POWs and a Medal of Honor recipient. There were helicopter pilots, a medic, some infantry soldiers, and others who made a career of the military and served in many capacities. Two among us had lost relatives. I roomed with the school nurse who served as a combination critical care facility and pharmacy.

As I had surmised, the experience was unlike my previous visits. None of the other vets had been back to Vietnam since their deployment over 40 years ago. Some had been very hesitant to make the journey, preferring to leave the past behind and not reopen old wounds. Others, like myself, were curious or felt a need to put closure to that chapter of their lives. As we crisscrossed the country, sometimes looking for nothing more than a bridge or road that had survived and could refresh a memory, tears welled up, nearly hidden beneath the bills of their commemorative hats. I was very interested in what effect returning for the first time would have on the men. As each stop on our journey unfolded, it seemed that they grew more comfortable with openly sharing their memories. After all, they were in the company of those who knew what they had seen, cared about what had transpired years ago, and were non-judgmental about their actions.

Surprisingly, it was me who had a flashback moment. It happened at the tunnels of Cu Chi. Work on these tunnels was begun during the French occupation and housed entire communities of Viet Cong in three underground levels. There were schools, medical facilities, and "offices" all functioning directly below some U.S. bases. In recent years, a few of the tunnels had been further hollowed out and dimly lighted to accommodate tourists wanting to get a sense of guerrilla warfare. One of the "attractions" there is the opportunity, at a cost of $1.50 US per bullet, to shoot an AK47 (Russian made firearm used by NVA) or an M-16 (carried by U.S. soldiers). During my previous visits, not many people chose to spend their money thus it was quite peaceful wandering through the wooded area. On this trip, however, a group of foreign tourists with change in their pockets, emptied bullet after bullet at the targets. The shots rang out shortly after we arrived, continued as we lowered ourselves into one of the tunnel entrances and lingered in the background while we crawled through the underground labyrinth. The damp, dark chill of the narrow passageways allowed the war to seep back into our souls. The pop, pop, pop in the trees made it all too real. I felt a lump rise in my throat as I started to cry! I wandered as far away as I could from the noise, but the tears would not cease. Knowing that it would be futile, I still pleaded with myself to stop. As some of the staff offered hugs of understanding all I could do was mumble apologies. After all these years and four return trips, the pain was still there.

Perhaps the most moving segment of the trip came

when our group toured the simple but poignant museum at Maison Centrale. When I first returned to Vietnam in 1994, demolition had begun on the building that had once housed American prisoners of war, including Senator John McCain. Like McCain and the two POWs in our group, many of those imprisoned there were pilots who had been shot down and captured by enemy forces. Among the many items displayed were thin straw mats, which the prisoners were supposedly given for sleeping, clean, neatly pressed clothing, eating utensils, cigarettes, sandals, and a box of Vicks Cough drops. Lining the walls were dozens of photos taken to portray the humane treatment that all of the prisoners supposedly experienced during their time at the HH. John and Bill set us straight with the truth. Food was scarce and sometimes inedible, beatings were routine, overcrowding was ubiquitous, and isolation unbearable. The two men did recognize some of the other POWs in the photos. Our group listened intently when they described how they created a somewhat complicated web of taps to spell out words in order to stay in touch with fellow prisoners. The system was fine tuned to allow nods or blinks of the eye to spell out words. Their resiliency amazed us all.

THE FINAL CHAPTER—FOR NOW

In my wildest imagination I could not have foreseen the wealth of opportunities that would be afforded me as a result of serving as an Army nurse for one year in a very unpopular war in a little known country. When asked about my personal feelings about the war, I repeat the same mantra each time, I would never wish for another war but would not change the experience that I had for anything. It is deeply entwined within the fiber of who I am. I chose not to ignore my past but rather to embrace it and share it in order that others may learn by the mistakes of Vietnam. I have addressed civic groups, hundreds of students from middle school level and above, veterans' organizations, and more. I have met some amazing individuals, made new friends, continued to travel, and even published photos and writings about the war. My effort to keep the tragedy of war in the public psyche will continue.

I will also fight for a cure for Parkinson's disease by sharing my story, while offering insight and listening to those also affected by this crippling condition. Whether a result of exposure to herbicides like Agent Orange (as in my case) or the result of some other factor, better treatment and a cure may soon be on the horizon. In the meantime, those of us who have adjusted to living with tremors, stiffness, poor balance, and depression, must assist others to live the best life that they can. That is a commitment that I made years ago and strive to fulfill every day.

As I face my 68th birthday, I have not lost that "wanderlust." I passionately look forward to many more opportunities to travel. (There are printed e-tickets in my desk drawer right now). Yet it was the Army and my youthful determination that gave me the incentive. I have definitely gotten to "see the world" and so much more.

| What I Fear Will Not Go Away

A slip of the foot on uneven paths
That strange ache in my leg as I write

The face, uneven, like a one-eyed queen
Shaking limbs, showing the world my imperfections

Thoughts meant to stir the soul to action,
Not yet in focus, needing to be recycled again and again

Love, not lost or lessened
Lust, buried deep, needing a GPS to locate it

Fear this? Fear tomorrow's advancing demons?
Sure! But what's to be done?

Grab fear and uncertainty by whatever presents itself
Hang on 'til life is wrestled from its grasp.

Take its energy; change its direction
Turn it within; transform it to hope.
Keep advancing and leave fear to find a new home!

| You Survived

*The shower of rockets at night The heat and monsoons
    during the day The fever and chills of malaria victims*

The tears of the wounded; the green bags for the dead.

You survived… The pleas of the amputee

Moaning with phantom pain The cries of injured children

Too young to understand; wanting only to be safe.

*You survived… Staring in the eyes of the enemy The
    loneliness without family nearby Food in the mess hall,
    powdered eggs and liquid Jell-O*

Sand in your face, on your sheets and your lips.

You survived…

*To return home, unbroken To go back to "The World,"
    unscarred*

You survived the war, though forever changed

By a silent villain called Agent Orange.

Playing my guitar on the beach

| My Guitar

Six nylon strings, sending mellow tones to those who would listen

Simple chords, to keep me on key—strummed, plucked, with or without capo, no pick

We would gather to forget the carnage of the day:

The dangling limbs held by tattered ligaments from blood soaked tourniquets

The acrid smell of burning flesh from white phosphorous.

Familiar strains to celebrate the quiet of the night sky unlit by flares

Searching for the enemy; revealing so much more.

Songs of love and loss, of sweat drenched nights and blood-smeared days

With others—singing, laughing, escaping, for there is comfort in community

Hot nights spent alone within four walls brings stress.

Monsoon drenched days, shared in the company of others, free the soul

There is joy in voices raised in song; relief in laughter

Healing the soul and preserving our sanity

Love of a different kind for those with uncertain futures

All brought together, by my war scarred guitar.

GLOSSARY

Agent Orange: Defoliant used in Vietnam

AK-47: Soviet-manufactured, semi-automatic and fully automatic combat assault rifle

APC: armored personnel carrier. A track vehicle used to transport Army troops or supplies, usually armed with a .50-caliber machine gun.

APO: Army Post Office located in San Francisco for overseas mail to Vietnam.

ARVN: Army of the Republic of Vietnam; the South Vietnamese Regular Army

AWOL: absent without leave; leaving a post or position without official permission

BOQ: bachelor officer quarters; living quarters for officers

Bronze Star: U.S. military decoration awarded for heroic or meritorious service not involving aerial flights

Bunker: fortified protection to withstand artillery strikes

C-130: large propeller-driven Air Force planes that carry people and cargo; the Hercules

C-rations: combat rations. Canned meals for use in the field. Each usually consisted of a can of some basic course, a can of fruit, a packet of some type of dessert, a packet of powdered coca, a small pack of cigarettes, and two pieces of chewing gum.

Civies: regular street clothes

DEROS: date of expected return from overseas. The day all American soldiers in Vietnam were waiting for.

DMZ: demilitarized zone. The dividing line between North and South Vietnam established in 1954 at the Geneva Convention

DOA: dead on arrival

Elephant Grass: tall, razor-edged tropical plant indigenous to certain parts of Vietnam

Flak Jacket: heavy fiberglass-filled vest worn for protection from shrapnel

Flashback: sense of dread recalling memories of the war

Frag wounds: puncture wounds caused by pieces of shrapnel which result from debris caused by an explosion

Hootch: a hut or simple dwelling, either military or civilian

HUEY: nickname for the UH-1 series helicopters. Commonly used to transport wounded

KIA: killed in action

Lambretta: three wheeled mini-bus for six passengers but often crammed with twice that many

Litter: stretchers to carry dead and wounded

LRB: little round boat used by fishermen

LZ: landing zone. Usually a small clearing secured temporarily for the landing of resupply helicopters. Some become more permanent and eventually become base camps.

M-16: the standard U.S. military rifle used in Vietnam from 1966 on. Successor to the M-14.

MARS line: Military Affiliate Radio Station. Used by soldiers to call home via Signal Corps and ham radio equipment.

Mas cal: mass casualty

Monsoon: period of weather when rain is constant and heavy

Mortar: a muzzle-loading cannon with a short tube in relation to its caliber that throws projectiles with low muzzle velocity at high angles.

MOS: military occupational specialty, specific job

MP: military police

MPC: military payment currency. The scrip U.S. soldiers were paid in.

NCO: non-commissioned officer, Usually a squad leader or platoon sergeant

NVA: North Vietnamese Army

OC: officers' club

PACEX: Pacific exchange—mail order service

POW: prisoner of war

PTSD: post traumatic stress disorder

Pungi Pit: hidden trap buried in ground filled with sharpened bamboo sticks

Purple Heart: award for being wounded

PX: Post Exchange

R & E: receiving and emergency

R & R: rest and recreation

Round Eye: non-Asian female

Shrapnel: pieces of metal sent flying by an explosion

Sniper: enemy who sneaks into fenced-in area by cutting barbed wire for purpose of shooting opponent

Steel Pot: helmet

TDY: temporary duty

Tet: Vietnamese New Year

Top Brass: highest level of military officers

Triage: determining the seriousness of each person needing medical treatment in an emergency room

USO: United Service Organization. Provided entertainment to the troops, and was intended to raise morale

VC: Viet Cong Communist led forces

APPENDIX

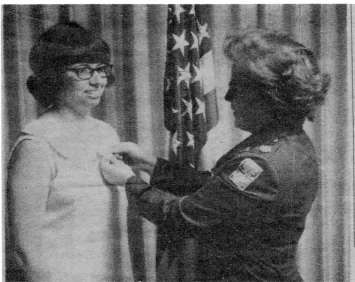

Belleville Star, Wed., May 31, 1967

Louise Graul   **Major Lee**

MASCOUTAH--Louise D. Graul receives her Army Student Nurse pin from Major Linda Lee, Army Nurse Counselor, after being sworn into the Army's Student Nurse Program in St. Louis.

Miss Graul, the daughter of Mr. and Mrs. Raymond J. Graul of 52 W. Patterson St., is a graduate of Mascoutah High School and is currently attending St. Joseph's School of Nursing in Alton.

As an Army Student Nurse, she will continue her nurses training at Alton with tuition and a salary paid by the Army.

Miss Graul entered the program through the Army recruiting station in Belleville.

Induction into the Army Nurse Corps 1967

SPECIAL ORDERS   25 May 1967
NUMBER   103   E X T R A C T

2.   TC 129.   Following individual having enlisted in USAR at US
Armed Forces Examining and Entrance Station, St. Louis, Missouri this
date for a period of four years for the purpose of participation in
the Army Student Nurse Program UP AR 601-19 and AR 140-111 is with
her consent ordered to Active Duty concurrently for the period indicated below, unless sooner relieved.   Effective on EDCSA indicated,
individual is relieved from assignment US Armed Forces Examining and
Entrance Station, St. Louis, Missouri and is reassigned to organization and duty station indicated.   TDN for FY 66/67 2172010 01-1151
P1411 S99-999.

GRAUL, LOUISE D   WR8591886   PFC E3   09D00

Assigned to: Stu Det (5002) Hq Fifth USA, Ft Sheridan, Ill 60037
               w/dy sta St. Joseph's School of Nursing, 915 E. Fifth
               Street, Alton, Illinois 62002
Will Proceed Date: 25 May 1967
Reporting Date: 26 May 1967
Date of Rank: 25 May 1967
Home Record: 52 W. Patterson, Mascoutah, Illinois 62258
Temporary Address: St. Joseph's Hospital School of Nursing, 915 E.
               5th St., Alton, Illinois 62002
Permanent Change of Station (MDC): 1-C
Date of Birth: 28 February 1947
Number of Dependents: None
Active Duty Commitment: 24 months
Basic Active Service Date: 25 May 1967
Basic Pay Entry Date: 25 May 1967
Expiration Term of Service: 24 May 1969
EDCSA (ENL): 25 May 1967
EDCSA (To report station): 26 May 1967

          FOR THE COMMANDER:

OFFICIAL: C. L. SHORTT
                                   CPT, AGC
                                   Adjutant

S. J. NOLES
2LT AGC
Asst Adjutant

Induction orders

137

DEPARTMENT OF THE ARMY
U. S. ARMY MEDICAL FIELD SERVICE SCHOOL
BROOKE ARMY MEDICAL CENTER
FORT SAM HOUSTON, TEXAS   78234

MEDEW-ZAR

14 JAN 1969

SUBJECT: Commendation for Superior Accomplishment

THRU: Commanding Officer
          Walson Army Hospital
          Fort Dix, New Jersey   08640

TO: Second Lieutenant Louise D. Graul, N5521848, ANC

1. On behalf of the faculty of the U.S. Army Medical Field Service
School, it is with pleasure that I congratulate and commend you for your
superior accomplishment while enrolled in the Army Medical Department
Officer Basic Course, 6-8-C20 (ANC, AMSC), from 14 November to 20 December 1968.

2. It should be of satisfaction to you to know that through your appli-
cation and contribution to the course, you graduated at the top of your
class and were designated as the Distinguished Honor Graduate. You were
awarded a certificate in recognition of this achievement.

                              O. Elliott Ursin
                              O. ELLIOTT URSIN
                              Brigadier General, MC
                              Commandant

Copy furnished:
Indiv pers rec jacket

Basic training commendation

138

EXTRACT

* * * *

108. TC 240. Fol rsg dir. FRAP AR 55-28. Indiv will send msg ntfy to CGUSARV advising of ch in ETA when trans scd are ch at transshpmt or stopover pt fol dprt from CONUS. Such msg WB given to CO of mil instl enr for xmsn. An ex bag alw of 134 lbs personal eff auth to acmp each indiv while tvl by acft. Cncr tvl of depn and shpmt of POV not auth. Clo rqr and tvl unif are presb in DA cir 700-17. UP par 11 AR 40-562 plague imm are rqr; tvl need not be delayed except for thr first vaccine dose. Indiv needing corr eye lenses WB equipped with mask protective fld M17 and nec corr eye lenses prior to dprt from CONUS. The introduction, pur and poss of privately owned wpn is prohibited in the Republic of Vietnam. WP. TDN. Instl comd will comply w/par 3c DA cir 600-57. CIC 201A01. MWBAS Personal Mail Sec APO San Francisco 96381. MCS 3449. Asg to USARV Tran Det APO San Francisco 96384 for fur asg. Aval date 30 Oct 1969 to arr OS dest NLT 3 Nov 1969. Scty clnc secret is rqr: resp comd comply w/AR 604-5. Lv data 30 DDALVAHP. PCS (MDC) 4A00. EDCSA 30 Oct 1969.

* * *

GRAUL, LOUISE D. ▆▆▆▆▆▆▆ 2LT ANC Walson Army Hosp
(W2JRAA-01) Ft Dix, NJ 08640. Aloc Nov-768 (IDC-4).

* *

MEYER, SHARON K. ▆▆▆▆▆▆▆ 2LT ANC Walson Army Hosp
(W2JRAA-01) Ft Dix, NJ 08640. Aloc Oct-2931 (IDC-4).

* *

275. TC 432. UP 10 USC 3914 (20-yr retirement) indivs rel fr act dy on EDCSA. On date immed fol EDCSA indivs are placed on ret list trf to USAR (Ret Res) and asg to USAR Cont Gp (Ret) USARC, St Louis, Mo 63132. SPN 230. HCSTWOY. PCS. TDN. PPSIA. MDC 7BE0.

Name, current grade, SSAN and MOS	EDCSA	Date retired	Place of retirement
SOTO, ANDRES (▆▆▆▆▆▆) SFC 94B4I68	30 Sep 1969	1 Oct 1969	Auth Ft Hamilton, NY, req Ft Dix, NJ.

BY ORDER OF THE SECRETARY OF THE ARMY:

W. C. WESTMORELAND,
General, United States Army,
Chief of Staff.

OFFICIAL:

Orders for Vietnam

DEPARTMENT OF THE ARMY
Headquarters US Army Training Center Infantry and Fort Dix
Fort Dix, New Jersey 08640

SPECIAL ORDERS   30 September 1969
NUMBER   273   EXTRACT

68. TC 370. Fol orders AMENDED.

SMO: Para 4 SO 245 Hq 3d Bn, 84th Arty APO NY 09176 dtd 7 Nov 68 AABY Para 1
      SO 270 Hq 3d Bn 84th Arty APO NY 09176 dtd 12 Dec 68
Pert to: RSG of SMITH, RICHARD M. ████████ CPT ARTY 1190 HHB 3d Bn 84th Arty
      APO NY 09176 asg to: USA ELM MACV APO SF 96384
As reads: Sp instr: Depn WB auth tvl to Hawaii for residence during Off
      tour IAW Para 43b(1)(a), Chap 9, AR 37-105 and para 13, Appendix II
      C 3, AR 55-46. Tvl of depn to Hawaii WB deferred until 15 Oct 69
      IAW 2d Ind DA Form 2370 HQ, USAREUR & 7A (ARAAG-PD) APO 09403
      dtd 6 Nov 68.
IATA: Port Call Data: Depn wife & two (2) dau will rept to Travis AFB, Fair-
      field, Calif NLT 1800 hrs 15 Oct 69 to board Flt No TKPB 2A1 dept O/A
      2000 hrs. Depn wife will have in poss DD Fm 1482 which may be secured
      from Trans Office.

SMO: Para 108 DASO 169 dtd 3 Sep 69
Pert to: RSG of GRAUL, LOUISE D. ████████ 2LT ANC US Walson Army Hosp, Ft Di
      NJ 08640 asg to: USARV Tran Det APO SF 96384 for fur asg.
As reads: NA
IATA: Port Call Data: Off will rept to Travis AFB, Fairfield, Calif NLT 1800
      hrs 30 Oct 69 to board Flt No TKPM 2B3 dept O/A 2000 hrs. Off will
      have in poss DD Fm 1482 which may be secured from Trans Office.

FOR THE COMMANDER:

OFFICIAL: JAMES W. LOVE
                                    Colonel, GS
                                    Chief of Staff

GENARO REYES-FLORES
CW3, USA
Asst AG

DISTRIBUTION:
100 - AHBOAG-OPB(Tvl Br)   2 - Postal O Ft Dix   1 - HQ FUSA ATTN: AHAAG-1
10 - AHBOAG-OPB   1 - AHBOAG-Mail Room
2 - AHBOAG-Files   1 - Ft Dix Off Open Mess
1 - AHBOAG   5 - CO, USA ELM MACV APO SF 96384
2 - AHBOGA   5 - CO, USARV Trans Det APO SF 96384
5 - AHBOFI   5 - CO, US Walson Army Hosp

Orders to report for flight to Vietnam

DEPARTMENT OF THE ARMY
HEADQUARTERS, US ARMY PERSONNEL CENTER
Fort Lewis, Washington 98433

SPECIAL ORDERS
NUMBER   280
EXTRACT

7 October 1970

448. TC 316. Following individual RELIEVED FROM ACTIVE DUTY as
indicated not by reason of physical disability, and ASSIGNED as shown
on date immediately following relief from active duty. All temporary
appointments held are terminated on your effective date of release.

GRAUL, LOUISE D ███████████ 1LT 3448 ANC
USATRFSTA (W1ZG03) Ft Lewis WA 98433

ADMINISTRATIVE ACCOUNTING DATA
Auth: By direction of the President, Sect XI and XIV Chap 3 AR 635-100
HOR: Mascouthah IL   OS-7-4
Mail adrs: 52 West Patterson Mascoutah IL 62258
PL EAD or OAD: St Louis MO
Last perm dy sta: APO 96325
SPN: 611
PCS MDC: 7B01
Eff date (REFRAD): 10 Oct 70

FOR THE INDIVIDUAL
Reserve grade, basic branch, component: 1LT ANC USAR
Assigned to: US Army Reserve Control Group (Reinforcement) US Army
              Administration Center 9700 Page Blvd St Louis MO 63132
Effective date of Reserve Assignment: 11 Oct 70
UMTS Act obligation: NA
Special Instructions: None

FOR THE COMMANDER:

J. A. ROEDER
1LT, IN
Asst Adjutant

STANLEY M. FOSCUE
MAJ, AGC
Adjutant

DISTRIBUTION:
C
30-Officer Concerned

Farewell to the Army

141

Becky Dylla and I visiting Mount Rushmore on our
Northwest trip post Vietnam, November 1970

ACKNOWLEDGMENTS

I must recognize Gary Swanson, who was among the first of my friends to suggest that I write a book about my time as an Army nurse serving in the Vietnam War. A couple years ago he even informed me that, should I write the book, he knew how I could get it published. Following through on that promise, he contacted Bob Babcock who then got in touch with me leaving me no choice but to write the book. Thank you Gary and Bob.

I also must say thank you to Caryn Mirriam-Goldberg, former poet laureate of Kansas and writing facilitator at Turning Point, the Center for Hope and Healing. Caryn's patience and guidance over the last several years have enriched my written word and given me the encouragement to keep on writing. Thank you to my daughter-in-law Gen Hillsburg for her suggestions along the way.

To all the teachers, community leaders, attentive students, and relatives who have sought to hear my story, I am most grateful. I never envisioned that, 45 years after I set out to "see the world," I would still be asked to share that experience.

To all my fellow Vietnam veterans, welcome home.

To Will and Emma—as you get older, should anyone

tease you by saying that your grandmother wore combat boots, proudly tell them, "Yes she did!" and hand them a copy of this book!

For just being there—Mary, Rita, Susan, and Jen

ABOUT THE AUTHOR

Growing up in a small Illinois town, Louise (Lou) Graul Eisenbrandt decided to join the Army in order to "see the world." After graduating as a Registered Nurse in June 1968, she attended basic training, then headed to Ft. Dix New Jersey, her first duty assignment.

In September 1969, she received orders for Vietnam, arriving there on November 1. During her year at the 91st Evac Hospital, she cared for GIs, South Vietnamese soldiers and civilians, and even Viet Cong and NVA soldiers. From malaria and hepatitis to double amputees, massive head traumas, and deadly bullet wounds; Lt. Graul saw it all.

Since 1970, she has made four return trips to Vietnam, the latest in September 2014, when she joined 11 other vets making their first return trip to the country.

For the past 30 years, the author has been sharing her experiences with students and community groups.

In addition, she is Chairman Emeritis of the board of Turning Point in Leawood, KS. Her other interests are travel, photography, golf, gardening, and finding a cure for Parkinson's Disease.

Lou lives in Overland Park, Kansas with her husband, Jim. They have two grown children and two grandchildren.

Vietnam Veterans and the College of the Ozarks come together for a memorable trip to Vietnam in September 2014

CPSIA information can be obtained at www.ICGtesting.com
Printed in the USA
LVOW02s1209230615

443413LV00005B/6/P